Robert Miles
and Annie Phizackle

White man's country

Racism in British politics

Pluto Press

London and Sydney

First published in 1984 by Pluto Press Limited,
The Works, 105a Torriano Avenue, London NW5 2RX
and Pluto Press Australia Limited, PO Box 199, Leichhardt,
New South Wales 2040, Australia

Cover designed by David Daniels

Computerset by Promenade Graphics Limited, Cheltenham

Printed in Great Britain by St Edmundsbury Press,
Bury St Edmunds, Suffolk

ISBN 0-86104-765-6

Contents

It is this whole complex – action and reaction – as well as what produced it and what its consequences were, which requires to be explained. We suggest that there is no simple 'event' here to be understood, apart from the social processes by which such events are produced, perceived, classified, explained and responded to.

S. Hall, *et al.*, *Policing the Crisis,* Macmillan: 1978, pp. 17–18.

It is not the people against whom we are discriminating tonight who are the problem in this country. It is the prejudice which has been directed towards them for certain motives.

Ben Whitaker, MP, *Hansard*, 1968, vol. 759, col. 1341.

Preface and acknowledgements

This book is about racism in Britain. It documents the growth of the expression of racism in British politics, and explains that growth in the context of the changing circumstances of British and international capitalism. We have written the book to make it readable and therefore of use to people who are just beginning their attempt to understand racism in Britain. Consequently, the text is not cluttered with notes and references, although there is a guide to further reading at the end which lists our major sources. We hope that the book will find a place on introductory courses in colleges and universities, in the trade union movement, and in any other educational process which deals generally with Britain and specifically with racism. If it does, we will feel that we have contributed something to the struggle against racism.

We believe that that struggle is now approaching a crucial stage. The racist bias of British domestic politics, which began in the 1950s, has reached the point where the conditions are now emerging for the realisation of the last major demand of the racists – the compulsory 'repatriation' of all West Indians and Asians in Britain. 'Strict immigration control' (meaning, in fact, 'keep the blacks out') had been achieved by the late 1960s, but the demands of, and support for, the racist cause have continued to grow. The escalating economic and political crisis of British capitalism since the mid-1970s has played a key role in the growth of that support. The 1979 general election was won by the Conservative Party partly as a result of its success in attracting the vote that had gone to the neo-fascist National Front in the course of the 1970s. The leader of the Conservative Party, Margaret Thatcher, made a carefully timed intervention in which she claimed that 'British people' had a legitimate reason to fear that their 'culture' might be 'swamped' by 'immigrants'.

As there are so few 'immigrants' whose entry need be controlled – thanks to the racist immigration laws – such a 'swamping' of 'culture' can be prevented only by the enforced removal of those people who currently legitimately and legally live their lives as an expression of their 'alien culture', as Margaret Thatcher, Enoch Powell and the National Front all put it. In a period of mass unemployment, and when those who are actively resisting the power of the state include some of these 'immigrants' (people who, in reality, are British-born children of West Indian and Asian parents with British citizenship), racism has the potential to become an even more powerful force.

The expression of racism fits neatly into the reactionary Conservative political package, founded as it is on an aggressive nationalism and support for a 'free enterprise' capitalism. The Conservative government, elected in 1979 and re-elected in 1983 on a similar programme, wants nothing less than the emasculation of the trade union movement and a major decline in working-class living standards as the price for capitalist recovery. The former is well on the way to being achieved through a combined policy of mass unemployment and legislation directed at the limited powers of the trade union movement; the latter is proving more elusive.

The ideology supporting and expressing this strategy is a radical one based on an explicit notion of 'Britishness', a concept which embraces past glories of industrial achievement and direct intervention in world affairs – by the use of force, if need be. The 'defence' of the Falklands (which inconveniently occurred at the same time as the Conservative government was busily stripping a proportion of its population of British citizenship) permitted the rekindling of some of those 'glories' of 'gunboat diplomacy'. The cost, in financial terms, was some £1 million per annum for each of the islands' residents.

The notion of Britishness also refers back to the past 'glories' of 'Empire' when Britain ruled the world, or at least the bits that 'gunboat diplomacy' had the power to retain. This rule was widely justified in terms of the benefits that British 'civilisation' would bestow upon the 'inferior races' of 'alien culture'. Such 'benefits' included a conception of 'sport' which identified the indigenous population of Australia as suitable targets for shooting along with other 'animals'. The memory of Nazi gas chambers is still sufficiently vivid to prevent explicit talk of 'racial inferiority' in post-1945 Europe on the part of the ruling class. However, imperial conceptions can be reproduced in a different form.

We now hear talk of the 'naturalness' of a people's desire to live 'amongst their own kind'. But the consequence is the same. When West Indians and Asians live in Britain they become the object of that talk and policy. The strategy cannot be seen in isolation from the aim of persuading the working class that their sacrifices are for the 'nation' when, in reality, they are for the benefit of capitalism and the ruling class. Racism is therefore an integral component of the Conservative government's ideology and approach.

There is a real sense in which this ideology and strategy are a radical departure from post-1945 politics. Nevertheless, the racist component does have some link with policies and practices pursued by previous post-war governments, both Conservative and Labour. Behind the rather weak and limited rhetoric of socialism, the Labour governments of the 1960s and 1970s played as important a role in the institutionalisation of racism in Britain as Conservative governments. This was not solely because these Labour governments were motivated by pragmatism and a policy of limited reforms to the capitalist system. It was also because the Labour Party's political philosophy is nationalist before it is class-based: it now always claims to speak for the 'British people' and to be a better interpreter of Britain's history and traditions than the Conservatives. Consequently, it is wide open to the strategy of speaking for the 'British people' as if they were a nation with interests opposed to 'other people's' – not least when those 'others' are of a supposedly different 'race'.

The outcome was a six-year period of Labour government in the 1960s when it competed with the Conservative Party over whether or not it really understood the feelings and interests of the 'British people'. In the process, it set up both the ideology and a large part of the structure of institutionalised racism which the subsequent Conservative government was able to rationalise in the form of the 1971 Immigration Act. In the course of that competition, it was confirmed to the 'British people' that the very presence of 'coloured immigrants' in

Britain was problematic. The Labour Party's 'change of heart' in the mid-1970s was not accompanied by the abolition of the 1971 Immigration Act in the lifetime of the 1974–9 Labour government, nor by a questioning of the by now common-sense notion that 'good race relations' were dependent upon 'strict immigration control'.

There is now a 25-year history of racist agitation within British domestic politics. All the demands of the racists, apart from compulsory 'repatriation', have been granted. Given the fact of mass unemployment and the Conservative government's attempt to instil a new consciousness of British heritage, it could be argued that the scene is now set for the Tories to 'bow' to increasing pressure and solve the former by 'repatriating' those in Britain who are not 'British'. After all, when Britain was 'great', the 'coloureds' were 'at home' and not here. If this seems an improbable outcome, it is worth reflecting upon the extent to which West Indian and Asian people have been allowed by the state to become the victims of physical attack and arson by neo-fascists while at the same time the state has identified these same people as the cause of Britain's so-called 'crime' and 'law and order problems'. If there ever was a 'liberal hour', it now seems many decades ago.

A book is always, to varying degrees, a collective enterprise and this is no exception. Many people have contributed to the preparation and writing in countless small and not so small ways. Rohit Barot and Tina Wallace have read and commented on various drafts at different stages, and have provided us with encouragement at those points when we were demoralised by the time and effort involved. Hugo Radice was supportive at our earlier stage in this book's long and varied career. Lesley Muirhead kindly read the text at very short notice and gave us a 'consumer's report' which proved very valuable. A prize for patience, persistence, gentle encouragement and a tough editorial line must be awarded to Richard Kuper. Pru Larsen helped at a crucial stage with typing. Our thanks go to all of them. Last, but most important of all, we thank Veronica and Steve for living with this project and the demands that it has made: at one point, Veronica translated much of our draft into legible text; both gave immeasurable support.

1. Racism and labour migration

Introduction

In May 1953, the House of Commons witnessed a parliamentary debate on whether or not to make racial discrimination illegal in the colonies. In the course of that debate, a Mr Beresford Craddock rose to speak against the motion which urged the Conservative government to eliminate the 'colour bar'. As part of his explanation for his opposition, he described Africans as follows:

> Let us remember that 95 per cent of them are primitive people. One of the reasons why they are not generally accepted into hotels is because their sanitary habits are not all that could be desired . . . It is well known that a large number of Africans in East and Central Africa are riddled with a disease of a very unfortunate kind . . . I will not dwell on that very delicate subject, but I think that Hon. Members who have experience will agree that the attitude of the African towards women and sexual matters is entirely different from the attitude of the general run of Europeans . . . it is a common practice among Africans to put children to sleep by the excitation of their uro-genital organs . . . The effect of alcohol upon an African is remarkable. I admit that sometimes alcohol has a remarkable effect on Europeans. But, speaking generally, alcohol seems to bring out all the evil instincts in the African in the most astonishing way . . . these views and practices are due to the psychological make-up of those primitive people from time immemorial.

For Craddock the populations of the African colonies, although British citizens in law, were not the same sort of human being as the British population. Rather they were 'primitive', inferior peoples, and therefore deserving of inferior treatment. Mr Craddock's speech was not loudly and enthusiastically supported by the Front Bench of the Conservative government, but the fact remained that HM's government was content to continue to rule over colonies where racial discrimination was a normal practice. Moreover, the motion was lost.

It is language, arguments and policies such as these which constitute a central dimension of British colonial history. That history provides the backdrop to the migration from the Caribbean and the Indian sub-continent which began in the early 1950s, not least because the 1948 British Nationality Act granted in law the right to enter, work and settle in Britain to all colonial and Commonwealth citizens. A large proportion of those migrants have become, in effect, permanent settlers and have produced children born in Britain. Collectively, these people have become defined as 'Britain's black population'.

Politicians somewhat more prominent than Beresford Craddock were, nevertheless, arguing in the 1960s and 1970s that these British citizens did not belong here and should be encouraged to 'go home'. Enoch Powell, MP, argued in a speech in September 1971:

> Of the great multitude, numbering already two million, of
> West Indians and Asians in England, it is no more true to say
> that England is their country than it would be to say that the
> West Indies, or Pakistan, or India are our country. In these
> great numbers they are, and remain, alien here as we would
> be in Kingston or Delhi; indeed, with the growth of
> concentrated numbers, the alienness grows, not by choice but
> by necessity.

As for the British-born children of these migrants, Powell was equally clear in his views on their 'alienness' in a speech in November 1968:

> Sometimes people point to the increasing proportion of
> immigrant off-spring born in this country as if the fact
> contained within itself the ultimate solution. The truth is the
> opposite. The West Indian or Asian does not, by being born
> in England, become an Englishman. In law he becomes a
> United Kingdom citizen by birth; in fact he is a West Indian
> or an Asian still . . . With the lapse of a generation or so we
> shall at least have succeeded – to the benefit of nobody – in
> reproducing in 'England's green and pleasant land' the
> haunting tragedy of the United States.

Moreover, like Beresford Craddock, Enoch Powell was opposed to any law which would make discrimination against these 'aliens' illegal. In April 1968, he was filled with much foreboding:

> This does not mean that the immigrant and his descendants should be elevated into a privileged or special class or that the citizen should be denied his right to discriminate in the management of his own affairs between one fellow-citizen and another or that he should be subjected to inquisition as to his reasons and motives for behaving in one lawful manner rather than another . . . The discrimination and the deprivation, the sense of alarm and of resentment, lies not with the immigrant population but with those among whom they have come and are still coming.

Powell has never made any public references to 'primitive people', but he is quite explicit in arguing that these migrants from the Caribbean and the Indian sub-continent are not like 'us' and should not be in Britain. In so doing, he both denies the reality and consequences of Empire (for there was a time when at least the British ruling class believed that the West Indies and India were 'ours') and the vast quantity of evidence which demonstrates that racism and discrimination are widespread in Britain. Nor does he consistently use the idea of 'race' to define what he sees as the problem, although his regular parallels with the United States are sufficient to ensure that his audience grasps what is to be understood by 'the problem'. But we refer to these arguments in order to demonstrate an important continuity in British history – the role of racism in defining who the British are supposed to be, by excluding from the category of 'us' those who have a different colour of skin. As Tom Nairn put it in 1970 (although, in his case, with reference to England rather than Britain):

> War was the great social experience of England in this century – yet war served only to confirm and revalidate the value of the past, to affirm the essential continuity of the national tradition. The only *new* experience, going sharply counter to tradition, has been that of the coloured immigration of the 1950s and 1960s. Hence, as Powell realised, it has become possible to define Englishness vis-à-vis this internal 'enemy', this 'foreign body' in our own streets.

We begin this book thus to indicate that what, in everyday common-sense terms, is now defined as Britain's 'race relations' problem is neither new nor, indeed, a problem of 'race relations'. The situation and events usually referred to as the 'race relations' problem are the outcome of racism and discrimination which have a long history, not only within Britain but also within the British Empire. In order to trace that history, we explain both why colonies were necessary and why migrants came to Britain in the 1950s and the 1960s. In both cases, the answer is to be found in the need by merchants and, later, by capitalists for workers to exploit and this involved the geographical movement of people. Hence, the main theme of our book is the relation between racism and labour migration. To define the problem in any other way is to obscure the historical record and the main features of the type of society in which we live.

This relationship receives no mention in common-sense definitions of 'the problem' and usually only secondary attention in the standard books on 'race relations' in Britain. The latter tend to concentrate first on a description of where the 'immigrants' have come from and of their culture, and, second, on the nature and extent of racial discrimination and its effects on the material and cultural circumstances of the 'immigrants' and their children. In order to explain why we have chosen not to write such a book, we will examine the official interpretation of Britain's so-called 'race relations problem'.

Common sense about 'race relations'

Politicians, newspapers and television constantly tell us that Britain has a 'race relations' problem. Ever since the 1960s, they have repeated, in unison and with great regularity, that the solution lies in immigration control. This has become common sense and hence, by definition, unquestionable. The following argument is familiar to most people in Britain:

> Of course, I don't mind them coloureds personally. I even work with some of them. It's just that there's too many of them. The government lets them flood in when we don't have enough jobs and houses for our own people. None of these riots would've happened if we'd kept the numbers down.

They should go to their own countries, stay with their own
kind.

The argument will usually be expressed in terms of sweet
reason. There is rarely any official mention of the 'primitive
people' or of the 'coloureds' being inherently or biologically
inferior or less intelligent, although such claims can be heard if
one persists too long in questioning this 'common sense'. What
is apparently being argued is that 'race relations' would not
have become a problem if the politicians had had the sense to
stop 'them' coming: without 'them', there would not be a 'race
relations' problem.

Having become accepted as common sense, this 'principle'
forms the basis for intepreting events. Thus, in the 1980s, it is
common sense that British people should object to the Asians
having jobs when they are unemployed. It is common sense that
British people should object to West Indian 'muggers' who live
off both the social security and attacks on old ladies. It is also
common sense that the police should take a tough stand against
rioters in 'black ghettos' and that immigration officers should do
everything possible to stop 'the coloureds' coming into the
country. Quite logically, it is now common sense to argue that
'they' should be sent back to where they come from, whether
they want to go or not.

In January 1978 Margaret Thatcher made a speech which
repeated the arguments voiced by Enoch Powell, just under ten
years earlier:

> If we went on as we are, then by the end of the century there
> would be 4 million people of the New Commonwealth or
> Pakistan here. Now that is an awful lot and I think it means
> that people are really rather afraid that this country might be
> swamped by people with a different culture. And, you know,
> the British character has done so much for democracy, for
> law, and done so much throughout the world, that if there is
> a fear that it might be swamped, people are going to react and
> be rather hostile to those coming in.

The logic of this interpretation seeks a solution to the problem
by first stopping the entry of West Indians and Asians and then
by agitating for their 'repatriation'. It means that those who are

the victims of widespread discrimination are transformed into the 'problem's' solution. Thus, this 'realism' literally turns the 'victim' into the 'cause' of his and her oppression. This means that discrimination within Britain is considered to be best solved by discrimination at the point of entry into Britain or (for those who benefited from the earlier 'mistakes' of politicians) at the point of exit. It is therefore no surprise that the 1976 Race Relations Act, which supposedly strengthened legislation against racial discrimination, does not apply to the decisions and actions of government. Hence, current immigration policy and practice keep West Indians and Asians out of Britain and yet allow large numbers of Canadians and Australians freedom of entry.

The problem is not the presence in Britain of people from the Caribbean and the Indian sub-continent, but the reaction to their presence: the problem is not 'them', but 'us'. The focus of study must be the proponents and practitioners of racism and discrimination, whether they be politicians, state officials or trade union activists. If we are to understand their beliefs and their practice, we need to investigate the conditions and circumstances in which they have enacted and enforced particular policies and legislation, or in which they have identified and pursued 'working-class interests'.

Such a focus means that certain outcomes and processes receive only secondary attention in this book. We neither begin with, nor document in any detail, the consequences of racism and discrimination for those who are its direct object. Nor do we detail the reaction and resistance to racism and discrimination on the part of those who are their object. This is partly because others have already done so, or are better equipped to do so, and partly because our aim is to transcend common sense about 'race relations' by a different theoretical approach. This relative silence does not mean that we deny or downplay the significance of the extent and effects of discrimination, or of the political reaction to those effects. The remainder of this chapter is devoted to an explanation of why we wish to offer an alternative to common-sense understandings of 'race relations' in Britain, and to an outline of an alternative theoretical and historical approach. The key terms of this alternative approach are racism and labour migration within the context of the uneven development of capitalism on a world scale.

Racism as ideology

In order to make sense of our argument that it is racism and not 'race relations' which is the real problem in Britain, we must first make clear what racism is. This is particularly important in the light of Margaret Thatcher's claim that it was 'natural' that British people should feel 'swamped' by 'alien cultures'. Hers was an endorsement of racism from the highest level and, as such, requires a clear response.

If something is said to be 'natural', it means that nature made it that way, that it cannot be altered. This is contradicted by that most fundamental characteristic of men and women – their capacity to organise themselves socially to overcome, even dominate, nature (as, for example, in the effort to obtain oil from the North Sea). Hence, forms of social organisation and ways of thinking are social products, the results of human activity, whether intentional or unintentional, in particular sets of circumstances. Racism, as an ideology, is one such social product. Its existence must therefore be explained historically, by searching for its origin in human activity in particular material contexts and by showing how it is reproduced in different contexts under changing conditions. The ideology of racism may now have many supporters and be part of common sense; it has not always been so.

What is meant by ideology and common sense? In the course of our childhood, education and work experience, we each gradually build up a picture of the social world and the way in which it works. We come to expect certain things to happen. We come to believe that certain things should be so. These beliefs and expectations constitute a sort of theory about how and why the social world is organised, an ideology. Over time, and for much of our daily lives, this ideology is not questioned or examined; it becomes taken for granted, common sense. Ideology and common sense are rarely organised or consistent. Each of the many beliefs, observations, values and expectations will conflict with some of the others. Nevertheless, they help each person to impose some sense of order and direction upon the social world.

Ideology is always the product of direct experience and of information passed on by others. The development of the media industry since the middle of the nineteenth century has provided a new and important source of information and meanings, and there have been many studies of its content and impact. These studies show that, despite the wide variety of information sources and competition between them, the messages that are produced are remarkably similar. Moreover, these messages tend to be supportive rather than critical of the existing society. Some of these studies have looked at the role of the media in the reproduction of racism. One of them studied newspaper reports in the 1960s which mentioned New Commonwealth migrants and their children. A number of different newspapers were included in the survey, reflecting the spread of editorial 'bias' in the newspaper industry.

The study showed, first, that despite different editorial 'biases', the newspapers tended to select the same stories to present as news. Second, it showed that a majority of the stories presented New Commonwealth migrants and their children as problems in one way or another. The stories concentrated on claims that too many 'immigrants' were coming into the country, that 'immigrant' women had a high birth rate and were draining the National Health Service, and that 'immigrants' were over-represented in criminal statistics. There were far fewer stories reporting the extent of racial discrimination faced by these migrants and their children. Third, the study showed that the stories' headlines used words associated with 'trouble' or 'conflict'. Fourth, it showed that newspaper editorials were contradicted by the actual reporting of news. Hence, it was common for editorials to highlight the discrimination faced by migrants, while the newspapers themselves carried stories which incorrectly presented a picture of 'immigration' as a never-ending flow of 'coloureds' into Britain. Finally, the study showed that the messages in the newspapers did directly influence the perception and opinions of those who read them. The result was that the overall, negative and hostile view of the migrants and their children was passed on to newspaper readers.

Such transmitted elements both affect and can be altered by direct experience: particular people and events can add new elements or change existing ones. But the real, practical problems that people have to face and overcome, and so the way in which the world is experienced, differ according to one's position in the class structure. Working-class people do not have to worry directly about the price of shares on the Stock Exchange or about guaranteeing the entry of their children into Eton. The rich do not have to worry about the price of bread and milk in the same way as people living below the poverty line. It is of such experience that ideology and common sense are partly made. Consequently, ideology and common sense should not be viewed as necessarily consciously 'made up' by a ruling class deliberately to confuse. Such an interpretation assumes that the working class is an empty vessel, waiting and willing to be 'filled up' with any convenient ideas. It denies that working people can test the ideas and interpretations that they receive from the government and the media against their own experience of the world. Ideology is not only 'handed down' (from one class to another, and from one generation to another), but is also constantly being created and renewed by people in response to the world as they experience it. Some elements of ideology are consciously created to confuse; others are a reflection of the world as it is experienced.

Finally, we consider ideology to consist of elements which are experienced as being true. That is, the component parts are, in the main, sincerely believed. However, taken as complete entities, ideologies are, from a scientific point of view, false. This is not so much because the world is wrongly interpreted and perceived (although this happens), but rather because the surface appearance of the world, as experienced, is not always an accurate guide to its underlying structure and process. Consequently, although particular elements of ideology may be domonstrably true, these coexist with a much larger number of elements which are not.

Knowing the ideology and common sense of an individual or class does not, by itself, tell us how that individual or class will act. Because ideology and common sense are rarely logical and systematic, they suggest or support contradictory courses of action. Moreover, elements of ideology and common sense are, potentially, prone to change as a result of being tested against new experiences and situations. Hence, when explaining what people and classes do, we must take account not only of their ideology but also of their material circumstances and situational pressures; these will be equally as important as determinants of action.

Although the object and some of the content of racism as ideology have changed over time, racism nevertheless exhibits a number of common features. Racism is an ideology which identifies individuals as belonging to a group on the basis of some real or imaginary biological or inherent characteristic. It is common for the group to be identified by reference to some immediately evident physical characteristic(s) – skin colour, size of nose, shape of forehead. However, in some instances, the group is attributed with some other characteristic, perhaps cultural – greed, for example – which is thought to be inherent in every member of the group. The group so identified by this biological or supposedly inherent characteristic(s) is then also defined as having some other social or psychological characteristic(s) which is regarded favourably. This combination of characteristics and evaluations is interpreted to indicate a difference, a 'race'. The ideology of racism additionally claims that all those who share these characteristics are necessarily deficient or inferior and so should be treated less favourably than other groups not so identified.

Racism can therefore constitute the foundation for discriminatory and unfavourable treatment of all individuals identified as belonging to the group. It can also be employed to justify such a course of action after it has occurred. In reality, it is often difficult to disentangle the ideology of racism from the practice of discrimination, although it is possible for each to occur without the other. For example, it is common enough to find someone who regularly tells his mates that he 'hates the blacks' but yet, when face to face with a West Indian fellow-worker, makes no attempt to treat him any differently. Alternatively, a person may have no clearly defined negative views about Asians (and may even explicitly claim that they do not hold racist beliefs) and yet will consistently ignore her Sikh neighbour in the bus queue every morning in favour of a conversation with Mr Harvey or Mrs Greenwood.

Racism is an element of the common sense of large sections of all classes in Britain. Within working-class common sense, racism rarely appears in the form of a structured argument but rather as a number of specific, often disjointed, claims – 'Them blacks, they're really thick', 'I wouldn't live next door to one. The coloureds have filthy habits.' It is common for contradictory claims to be made – 'Them blacks come over here and take all our jobs', 'I reckon the coloureds should be sent back: they only come here to live on the dole and peddle drugs.'

Within the dominant class, one rarely hears such views publicly expressed. Even in 1954, Beresford Craddock was something of an exception and today it is very rare to hear public talk of 'primitive people' and the supposed 'racial superiority of the white man' outside the ranks of the neo-fascist organisations. The new racism of the dominant class has, however, an intimate relationship with these explicit claims 'from below', because they are first defined as 'legitimate fears'. It is then argued that it is 'natural' and 'instinctive' for people to feel that they belong to a 'nation' and for them to be hostile to a group with an 'alien' culture. Only rarely is the word 'race' overtly used. The idea though, remains: the world's population is divided 'naturally' into different groups, and this division is expressed in different cultures, each with its own geographical location and contribution. This theory serves to endorse the claim made by a working-class man we interviewed in London in the mid-1970s:

> The Londoners are moving out into the country because it's
> the only place they can live nowadays. I got nothing against
> them. There's too many of them. They run the transport.
> They can get houses from the Council. I can't. My mum said
> I would make a fortune if I was black.

This is a racism appropriate to a situation where the 'alien' is now within. It could never have served at the time when the 'British character' was doing 'so much throughout the world' by not only being in 'other people's countries', but also by justifying British rule (not to mention the 'repatriation' of profits) over them by reference to 'their primitive character'.

New Commonwealth migration and the idea of 'race'

Before 1945, the main expressions of racism concerned the Irish and the Jews, although there is a long history of racism directed against that small number of 'black' people who made Britain their home. The expression of racism in Britain since 1945 has focused primarily upon people who migrated to Britain from certain former British colonies which obtained political independence in the post-war period. Collectively, these colonies are called the New Commonwealth in order to distinguish them from those colonies which had obtained independence much earlier – Canada, Australia and New Zealand. (This Old Commonwealth also included South Africa up until 1960.) By the mid-1960s, the New Commonwealth included India, Pakistan and a number of Caribbean islands, notably Jamaica, Trinidad and Barbados.

Migration from the New Commonwealth to Britain began in the early 1950s in direct response to shortages of labour in certain sectors of the British economy: these men and women from the Caribbean and the Indian sub-continent who came to sell their labour power for a wage in British factories, hospitals and transport industries were no more or less than migrant labour. But, for large sections of the British population, what was significant about them and their presence was their physical appearance – or rather, the difference in their appearance when compared with 'ours'. The prime, but not the sole, measure of this difference was identified as skin colour: they were 'coloured'. The fact of physical difference signified that 'they' were of a different human species, a different biological type. That boundary was described as a difference of 'race'. Put another way, these migrant workers from the New Commonwealth were racialised in the domestic context. We use this notion of racialisation to refer to a historical process in which the idea of 'race', and its use to describe particular populations, is ultimately connected with colonial exploitation.

The idea of 'race' placed relations between indigenous and migrant populations into a quite distinct category, one in which physical differentiation was considered to take precedence in explaining those relations. The migrants were, therefore, always 'black' or 'coloured' before they were workers, neighbours, mothers, trade unionists, or even just people. But these migrant workers were not even just a 'race' apart: it was not only that 'they' were not the same type of human being as 'us' (although that was significant enough). It was also that 'they' were migrants from the British Empire. The very existence of Empire was viewed historically, the outcome of the struggle between superior and inferior 'races', an outcome in which the labour of the inferior 'races' had been appropriated not only to ensure 'their' advancement towards 'civilisation' but also, and especially, 'our' advancement to the position of *Great* Britain, workshop of the world. Or so it was thought. Hence, the migrant worker from Jamaica or India was already thought of as the descendant of slaves or coolies, forms of labour viewed as both inferior and troublesome. Moreover, the break-up of Empire which began in the 1950s provided yet further evidence for the inferiority of the colonised 'races', not least in the form of military conflict and dictatorship in Africa. The association of physical difference with negative attributes in a deterministic manner in the minds of sections of all classes in Britain meant that the reaction to the migrants was racist.

The vast majority of us have been brought up to believe, as common sense, that the world's population is naturally divided into a number of distinct 'races', each biologically and culturally distinct from the others. The crudest, and most widely known, classification is that between Caucasian, Negro and Mongoloid 'races'. The measure of 'race' is thought to be in real, objective physical differences, differences that we can all see. 'Race', it *seems*, is obvious. Unfortunately, it is one of the human species's most dangerous myths.

This is demonstrated in two ways. First, it is the case that only certain physical features are thought to indicate a difference of 'race'. Within any group of people there are differences of hair colour, height, weight, colour of eyes, length of arms, and so on. Any one of these physical features could be the basis for dividing these groups into biological categories, in the same way that skin colour is used to divide human beings into biological categories.

All these physical differences, including skin colour, are real and objective (although they are not fixed, but change over time). They are all *obvious* in the sense that they can be directly observed. But only some of them are *seen*: when a person is identified as being of a different 'race', it involves a process of selective perception, a honing in on *some* of the wide range of physical differences. 'Races', then, do not naturally exist; they are socially created by human beings. 'Race' is not an objective, biological feature; it is an idea. The human species is not naturally divided into discrete and distinct biological 'races'; it has divided itself into what is believed to be 'races'. Hence, 'races' only exist insofar as people think, and behave as if, they exist.

This conclusion is supported by the historical evidence: the idea of 'race' is historically very recent and emerged specifically in Western Europe. The word 'race' first appeared in the English language, in the early sixteenth century, as a synonym for a group or class of things. Subsequently, it was used to refer to a particular group of people who were thought to have a common history and experience. It was only from the later eighteenth century onwards that the word 'race' was used to identify groups of people who were thought to be biologically distinct. This meaning developed in the context of the growth of the biological sciences. The scientists of the day were attempting to classify plants and animals into different 'families' or species and *homo sapiens* (who, from a biological point of view, was just another animal) was not exempted from this process. The product of their 'scientific' investigations was a number of classifications of the world's human population into different biological types, or 'races', on the basis of certain physical differences. Moreover, it was also argued that some of these 'races' were biologically and culturally superior to others.

The fact that different scientists produced different classifications of the world's supposed 'races' suggested that such classifications were indeed arbitrary and non-scientific. Moreover, the idea that the human population was divided into fixed, physical groups became difficult to maintain against the theory of evolution and, later, of genetics. Subsequent work by geneticists in the twentieth century has shown that although there are genetic variations between different sections of the world's population, these differences do not coincide with 'race' divisions; neither are those differences fixed and absolute. In the wake of the Nazi Holocaust, during which six million Jews in Europe were slaughtered, the United Nations Educational, Scientific and Cultural Organisation gathered together a group of the world's best scientists. They met in Paris in 1949–50, and their conclusions included the following:

> The scientific material available to us at present does
> not justify the conclusion that inherited genetic differences are
> a major factor in producing the differences between the

cultures and cultural achievements of different peoples or
groups . . . For all practical social purposes 'race' is not so
much a biological phenomenon as a social myth. The myth of
'race' has created an enormous amount of human and social
damage.

This argument was subsequently confirmed by further
gatherings of scientists organised by UNESCO in 1951, 1964
and 1967.

The fact that scientists made a major error suggests that there
were influences on their work which were distinctly non-scientific. The work of these scientists, the issues with which they
were concerned and the ways in which they thought about
them, were all shaped by the economic and political context of
the time. One important dimension of that context was the
debate over slavery. Those merchant-capitalists with interests
in sugar plantations and trade in the Caribbean were under
attack for their use of slave labour; they desperately needed a
justification for this form of labour by the late eighteenth century. The same issue was raised again by the American Civil
War in the middle of the nineteenth century. The supposed
natural inferiority of the so-called 'Negro race' was more than
adequate for the task, as indeed it was to one side of the argument over the extension of the British Empire in Africa in the
later nineteenth century. These events did not, in themselves,
cause the scientists to produce a theory of 'race', but they were
widely known and discussed topics amongst the class to which
many of these scientists belonged. They were therefore one of
the major influences on the production of a theory that we can
call scientific racism.

Although the world's scientists now recognise that an error
was made, this understanding has not made much impact upon
everyday common sense. The reasons for this are complex. It is
the case that the idea of 'race' has a certain practical adequacy
in making sense of certain patterns of physical difference which
are there for everyone to see. More importantly, the populations who were racialised in the eighteenth and nineteenth centuries have continued to be the object of concern and policy on
the part of the dominant class in Britain and, more generally, of
Western capitalism. The liberation struggles in Africa and
South-East Asia, the case of apartheid in South Africa and the

resistance to racism in the United States in the 1950s and 1960s were all matters which directly affected the economic and political interests of the dominant class and ensured that major political and media attention was paid to them. More specifically, and in relation to our concern here, when sectors of British industry ran short of labour in the 1950s, it was recruited and encouraged to come from parts of the world which had been colonised and racialised in the preceding centuries. Upon arrival in Britain, the migrants were immediately understood, not in terms of their common humanity, but by reference to a particular set of physical characteristics that had previously been associated with a set of negative meanings. They were therefore understood as a 'race' (or, sometimes, 'races') apart.

Similarly, 'race relations' are not naturally occurring social relations between biologically distinct groups. Rather, only certain sorts of social relations in certain situations come to be understood as 'race relations'. Like 'race', 'race relations' is a label which is applied in particular circumstances, and we therefore have to explain why this is so.

Capitalism, colonialism and labour migration

'Race' came to have its contemporary meanings within capitalist society. Three features of the system are particularly relevant. First, before capitalist production can begin, there has to be an initial accumulation of wealth in the hands of a minority. This is the outcome of a complex historical process: in England, it included the setting up of the colonial system which involved the transfer of a large quantity of wealth from the Caribbean and from India to England. From the late seventeenth century until the early nineteenth century, English interest in the Caribbean centred on the production of sugar and rum by means of slave labour. India became important only in the eighteenth century – first as a source of tribute, and later as a source of raw material (cotton) and as a market for the manufactured goods produced using this raw material. Thus, the colonial system involved different forms of colonial exploitation. Whereas in the Caribbean English economic interests necessitated the creation of a particular type of society based on slavery, in India a long-established society and mode of economic organisation were subordinated to English economic and political control.

Second, the development of capitalist production requires the development of a world division of labour: if Lancashire was to be the site of cotton production, then it must be supplied with raw material. In the early half of the nineteenth century, it was supplied from the southern half of the United States which produced cotton with slave labour.

Third, in particular periods of major capitalist expansion and accumulation, the supply of labour within the nation-state where that capital is located does not keep up with the demand. One way of solving this problem is to encourage labour migration: migrant labour, or those who move from one geographical location to one where expanded production is taking place, can be attracted only if the area from which they move cannot offer paid-wage labour or cannot offer wages as high as those offered elsewhere.

In the case of Britain, these three features have been intimately connected. For example, one of the locations for the early accumulation of capital was the Caribbean. Initially important as an area from which to attack and rob Spanish ships returning from South America, the British Caribbean islands were later developed to take their place as one of the world's leading suppliers of sugar: profit was obtained not only from the production of sugar cane, but also from the means by which labour was obtained to grow sugar cane – the slave trade. We now know that some of that profit was accumulated to finance the so-called industrial revolution which began in the latter half of the eighteenth century. The pre-eminent position of the Caribbean islands in the world division of labour was, however, temporary and as other suppliers and sources of supply became more important, those who had provided the labour power were no longer required. As British interest in developing the Caribbean declined, so did the islands' economic and social condition. Their economies had been a short-term, artificial creation which were unable to maintain any autonomous economic development after British investment was reduced. The population, formally freed from the bonds of slavery, became trapped in less obvious, but no less powerful, chains. Faced with the problems of obtaining the means to live and a cash wage, they opted for migration in search of paid work.

Labour migration became a tradition in the British Caribbean from the end of the nineteenth century, the flow being dependent upon a demand for labour somewhere else in the world. At the turn of the century, the building of the Panama canal provided such a demand, as did growing industrial cities of the northern United States – at least up until the 1920s. After 1950, both capitalists and the state in Britain found themselves short of labour in particular sectors, and so another phase in the history of labour migration from the Caribbean opened.

It has been the uneven development of capitalism which has provided the underlying dynamic for many of the large-scale migrations of people over the past three centuries, from the 9 million Africans transported as slaves to the Americas, to the 12 million southern European and colonial migrants who were working as wage labourers in the economies of north-west Europe in the late 1960s. Though the nature and degree of compulsion involved in these two examples differ, the common factor remains the interaction between capitalist development and the demand for labour in particular geographical locations.

What was required was cheap labour power; only secondarily was attention given to the increase in the supply of housing, educational and social security resources that must accompany any increase in the working population. Indeed, it was rarely envisaged that such resources should be made available to migrants on the same terms and to the same (usually inadequate) degree as they were to workers born within the nation-state. In the longer run, of course, the migration inevitably increased the demand for resources and facilities already in short supply. It is within this sort of framework that racism has had, and continues to have, its effects.

Against common sense

By the early 1960s the overriding feature of the political and ideological reaction to Indian and Caribbean migrant labour was racism. Not only were the migrants considered to be a 'race' apart but, in addition, this was a mark of their inferiority which justified their exclusion from equal access to jobs, housing, education and other facilities and resources. Seen in this way, the problem is very different from that suggested by politicians and the media.

First, it is a problem of racism: our attention should not be primarily focused on the migrants and their culture (their religion, mode of dress, diet, etc.), but on the reaction to them of employers, the state, the trade unions, and the working class. In the case of Britain since 1945, this means that our focus is on the domestic racialisation of colonial migrant labour. Second, labour migrations can only occur in the form that they do because labour power is only another commodity, to be bought and sold on the market. Capitalists never want people, only their capacity to labour: they become concerned with people only insofar as a lack of concern would threaten the supply of labour power. The migration of people to ensure that labour power is made available in particular centres of production is a central feature of the way in which labour power functions as a commodity in a capitalist society. It is because labour power is a commodity that there is the space for racism to define some suppliers as less than human; it is because of labour migration that there is a circulation of persons with a wide range of cultural and physical features who cannot meet as human beings but as sellers of labour power. For these two reasons, the second dimension of the problem in Britain is that it is a capitalist society.

The structure of the book follows directly from this alternative to the common-sense notion of a 'race relations' problem in Britain. The first part deals with the political and ideological reaction within Britain to the migration of labour from the New Commonwealth – with what we call the racialisation of British politics. We go on to place this process of racialisation in the wider context of the relationship between capitalism and labour migration, both within Britain and internationally. Finally, and only within this framework, we consider the implications of racism and discrimination for the migrants themselves, and for our understanding of the British class structure and class struggle.

2. The construction of the 'race/immigration' problem: 1945–62

Introduction

Only certain issues and events come to be defined as political problems requiring attention and action, but there is no necessary logic or validity to the process by which this happens. It is therefore possible for one situation or event to be consistently ignored by politicians and the media, while another is the consistent object of political attention despite the fact that, objectively, the former has greater negative consequences than the latter.

For example, strikes are defined as a problem which requires political attention in the form of legislation. Since 1945, both Conservative and Labour governments have made various attempts to reduce the number and effects of strikes. Government priorities are reinforced by the activities of journalists who consistently select strikes as objects of 'news' and present them as the outcome of 'agitation' or 'irrationality'. One of the commonly stated reasons to justify this emphasis is that strikes mean lost production and, hence, reduced profits, lost markets and fewer jobs. The argument is that strikes create problems for everyone, and so are a problem for everyone. Yet more work days are lost through industrial accidents than through strikes. So, if we accept the justification for concern about strikes, we must expect to hear even greater concern about industrial accidents. In fact, the very opposite is the case. It is not only that certain issues and events are ignored in favour of others in the creation of political problems; even where there is some sort of consensus about the significance of an issue or event, there can be competing definitions of why it is significant. This is not simply a matter of conflicting explanation, but also of the very language used in the identification of the issue or event and in the explanation of its significance and occurrence. For example, there is general acceptance that the situation in Northern

Ireland is problematic, but there is widespread disagreement on the nature and origin of that problem. For the Conservative and Unionist forces, the issue is one of 'law and order' and 'terrorism' in a context where the majority of the population wish to remain part of the United Kingdom. For the Republican and socialist forces, the problem is foreign occupation by the British state of Ireland in a context where majority opinion was gerrymandered by the way in which the 1922 boundary between the Republic of Ireland and Northern Ireland was drawn to ensure a permanent Protestant majority.

Hence, when we are told that an issue or event is a political problem, we must ask how it has been so defined. This involves identifying the various individuals, groups and organisations who have been involved in the process, and the ways in which they have defined the problem. Frequently, these various participants will have been engaged in a political struggle to ensure that one view prevails over another, as well as an ideological struggle to ensure that that view or definition has a particular content. These political and ideological struggles, and the way in which they are resolved and recur, will have real consequences. Thus, the fact that industrial accidents are not widely defined as a political problem requiring legislative intervention means that men and women will continue, quite needlessly, to be killed at work.

It is now widely believed in Britain that the country has a 'race' problem as a result of 'immigration'. How was this notion of 'race/immigration' constructed as a problem requiring political action in the early years of labour migration from the New Commonwealth? There was nothing new or special about either a shortage of labour in British capitalism or a migration of people to supply labour power, as we shall see later. What was new and special in Britain in the post-1945 period was that the people who migrated to fill the demand for labour were, upon arrival, defined as an inferior 'race'. Moreover, it was argued that the relations of 'race' between the 'coloureds' and the British (i.e. the 'whites') were the consequence of immigration. Thus, when those 'race relations' came to be defined as problematic, political attention came to focus on 'immigration' as a means of solving that problem. One central ideological consequence of this was that the notions of 'race' and 'immigration' became interchangeable, and so, whenever 'immigrants' and 'immigration' became the centre of debate, the reference was in fact to 'coloured people', regardless of their place of birth, and not to *all* persons entering Britain.

The 'race/immigration' problem as common sense

The notion of a 'race/immigration' problem has a certain common-sense logic. The idea of 'race' is premised on the assumption that the world's population is divided naturally into discrete biological types, each having distinct qualities and abilities suited to its particular circumstances and geographical situation. Having accepted this assumption, it does follow that 'races' will only come into contact with one another as a consequence of geographical movement, or 'immigration'. This common-sense conclusion is, however, completely mistaken. In the first place, and as we have already shown, the idea of 'race' has no scientific justification. Second, the term 'immigration' refers to the movement of persons from one country to another with an intention of permanent settlement. In fact, the majority of these who came to Britain in the 1950s and 1960s from the New Commonwealth rarely had such an intention. Rather, they wanted to stay for a relatively short period, in the course of which they hoped to save a sufficient sum of money in order to return 'home' and improve their material and social circumstances there. Most of these people were young and single and, in the case of those from the Caribbean, were drawn equally from both sexes. These people were, in fact, migrants who had temporarily left their country of birth to find work and a wage. Viewed from the 1980s, these migrants have now become permanent settlers; this, however, was largely the outcome of events and circumstances *after* the migration. Ironically, one of the reasons for this change was the introduction of controls over the entry of Commonwealth citizens – the early migrants were forced to make a choice about where they would begin and maintain family life.

In an absolute sense, then, there was no 'race/immigration' problem in Britain in the 1950s. Rather, migration of labour from the New Commonwealth to Britain was made an object of political attention, as a result of which the ideological notion of 'race/immigration' came to be used to identify the consequences of this labour migration. Hence, what was problematic was not the migrants but those who were actively engaged in identifying the migrants as a problem. Moreoever, by focusing on the physical appearance of the migrants, and by linking features such as skin colour with a negative evaluation of the migrants (it was commonly alleged, for example, that 'they bring disease into the country and cause crime'), this construction and use of the 'race/immigration' notion was itself racist.

The remainder of this chapter describes how this racist reaction to labour migration from the New Commonwealth was constructed and reproduced in the 1950s. In this period, a number of individuals and groups within both the state and the labour movement were able to develop a political campaign which, in a context where the state proved itself unwilling to provide the material resources for an increase in the labour force, was able to claim with some validity that it spoke for a large proportion of the 'British people'. And it was in this period that, if the state and the labour movement had acted and reacted differently, the problem could have been identified for what it really was, one of racism.

' . . . Of good human stock'

One of the bigger political fears in the immediate period after the end of the Second World War was a return to mass unemployment. The election of a Labour government in 1945 implied that the situation of the 1930s would not be allowed to recur, and it certainly did not. This was due not so much to Labour Party policy in itself, but to the adaptation of the capitalist economy to conditions of peace. This adaptation and growth quickly revealed labour shortages in certain sectors of the economy and a number of private and state recruitment schemes for migrant labour were established. Between 1946 and 1950, 77,000 displaced persons from Eastern Europe were brought to Britain as European Volunteer Workers and placed in essential industries with labour shortages such as agriculture, coal-mining, textiles, clothing, foundries, etc. A further 8,000 Ukrainian prisoners of war were likewise placed and approximately 88,000 members of the Polish Armed Forces who did not wish to return to Poland were helped settle in Britain and placed in employment during this period. While other official recruitment schemes of foreign workers (mainly of Italians and Germans) involved much smaller numbers, the actual number of aliens landed with work permits between 1946 and 1950 totalled 136,000, including dependants. Thus little attention was paid to the arrival in 1948 of some 400 people from the West Indies on the *SS Empire Windrush*, all of whom came in search of work, although the Colonial Office did monitor the repercussions. But, with its commitment to planning and the varied effects of almost six years of war, the government set up a Royal Commission to report on the British population.

The Royal Commission's report was published in 1949. One of the problems it identified was the possibility of a shortage of labour in certain sectors of industry where the conditions of work were unattractive. It estimated that some 140,000 young people might have to migrate to Britain annually in order meet the shortfall, and noted that this would necessitate considerable expenditure on housing and social services as well as industrial training. But, for the Royal Commission, the problem was not simply one of capital expenditure. There was also a problem of who these migrants were to be. The commission believed that there was little possibility of attracting such large numbers of people from Europe, including Ireland, which had been the main source of labour for British capitalism in the nineteenth century. The commission continued:

> Immigration on a large scale into a fully established society
> like ours would only be welcomed without reserve if the
> immigrants were of good stock and were not prevented by
> their religion or race from intermarrying with the host
> population and becoming merged in it.

Hence, 'the sources of supply of suitable immigrants for Great Britain are limited, as is also the capacity of a fully established society like ours to absorb immigrants of alien race and religion.' The commission concluded that 'large-scale immigration' was both undesirable and impracticable. Explanation and justification for these claims and conclusion were notably absent, but the ideology of 'good stock' and 'race' implied that Britain's future labour shortage was not to be solved by 'coloured immigrants'.

In the 1950s, however, employers proved themselves to be less concerned with religion and 'race'. 'Large-scale immigration' became a reality, despite the conclusions of the Royal Commission's report, because sections of British capitalism decided that they could not maintain production without it. But if economic factors were decisive in this respect, political and ideological backing was far from absent. The British Nationality Act (1948) had implicitly confirmed that the Commonwealth was a potential source of labour by defining all Commonwealth citizens as British citizens, with the right of entry and settlement in Britain. This was well understood by those employers who paid for recruiting advertisements in the West Indies, India and Pakistan throughout the 1950s. The fact that the Royal Commission failed to recognise these British citizens as a potential source of labour confirms the suspicion that such people were considered not to be 'of good stock'.

The Royal Commission's concerns were expressed with increasing intensity and regularity in the course of the 1950s within the state, although the language was not always so explicit.

Mutterings and discontent inside the House

The *SS Empire Windrush*'s arrival from Jamaica excited little political interest. A small number of Labour MPs asked a number of parliamentry questions through June 1948, but their main concern was whether or not the government would assist the West Indians to find work and accommodation and would ensure that they did not have to face any discrimination. There was no suggestion that they were not 'of good stock', but rather a full awareness that these were British citizens who had the right both to be in Britain and to be treated as such. However, this view was not shared by all, and within the Cabinet of the Labour government there was support for the idea of racist immigration control. A Cabinet committee was set up to review the 'means which might be adopted to check the immigration into this country of coloured peoples from the British colonial territories'. The committee reported to Cabinet in February 1951, and recommended that no action be taken at that time. It was, however, very concerned about how controls might be applied in the future if the charge of racism was to be avoided:

> Any solution depending on an apparent or concealed colour test would be so invidious as to make it impossible of adoption. Nevertheless, the use of any powers taken to restrict the free entry of British subjects to this country would, as a general rule, be more or less confined to coloured persons.

The fact that a Labour government (and one generally regarded as the most radical of all Labour governments) was prepared even to consider this option means that we should not be surprised by the activities of certain right-wing Conservative MPs in the course of the 1950s.

The major role was played by two Conservative MPs, Cyril Osborne (Louth) and, after 1955, Norman Pannell (Liverpool, Kirkdale) who, in a regular series of parliamentary questions, sought to identify New Commonwealth migrants as criminals and carriers of disease. Although on several occasions they claimed to be concerned with controlling all immigration, the object of their questions was invariably West Indian migrants. Moreover, their own questions did reveal their racist motivation. For example, on 24 January Cyril Osborne asked the Conservative prime minister:

> What is Her Majesty's government's policy regarding the increase in emigration of young British men and women with high scientific qualifications, and the corresponding increase in immigration into this country of coloured people without tests of either health, technical skill or criminal record; and in view of the recent increase in unemployment, what action the government proposes to take, and what co-ordinating measures are to be taken?

Osborne and Pannell's campaign was representative neither of Conservative policy nor of general opinion amongst Conservative MPs at that time. The same is also true of those Labour MPs who wanted to draw attention to the West Indian presence in Britain. On 5 November 1954, John Hynd (Sheffield, Attercliffe) initiated an adjournment debate on what he defined as the problem of the increased numbers of 'coloured colonial immigrants' entering Britain who, in his view, had no prospects of employment or of finding accommodation. Hynd acknowledged that they were British citizens with the right to enter Britain, but continued: 'there are several hundred millions of British subjects of different races and colours in various parts of the world, and it would not be possible to accept the implications of that argument if the problem got out of hand.' For him, the problem was clearly the increasing numbers of 'coloured colonial immigrants' coming to Britain. The 'ticklish question' identified by Hynd was therefore one of controlling the entry of these 'coloured colonial immigrants', but in such a way that 'will not affect the principle of the right of these people to come to a country whose citizens they are'. In effect, he was saying that 'coloured colonial immigrants' could retain the right to enter Britain, but should be prevented from exercising it.

The manner in which he continued his speech suggested that he was half-aware of being open to the charge of racism because he made such great efforts to deny that the problem was anything to do with a 'colour bar' in Britain. Eventually, the difficulty of maintaining the pretence proved impossible:

> Neither is the problem in the dance halls, where incidents
> have occurred in our provincial towns. In many cases a part
> colour bar has had to be imposed against people of a certain
> colour or type . . . It is a pity that such things have to be
> done, but that is not a colour bar . . . These matters have to
> be properly understood. Much of the talk about a colour bar
> should be dropped.

Presumably, it would also be a misunderstanding to identify Hynd's call for a restriction of the right of entry of 'coloured colonial immigrants' as a 'colour bar'.

Henry Hopkinson, Minister of State for Colonial Affairs, replied on behalf of the government. He confirmed that British subjects from the colonies had the right to enter Britain and continued:

> This is not something that we want to tamper with lightly. In
> a world in which restrictions on personal movement and
> immigration have increased we still take pride in the fact that
> a man can say *civis Britannicus sum* whatever his colour may

be, and we can take pride in the fact that he wants and can
come to the Mother country.

As for whether or not there was a problem, the minister took
a sanguine view. He claimed that there was no evidence of a
'colour bar' in Britain (so passing over in silence Hynd's reference to dance halls) and no evidence of difficulty for the West
Indian migrants in obtaining jobs. However, he did concede
that there were problems arising from the pre-existing housing
shortage, which had led to a concentration of migrants in sub-
standard housing; he believed that this was a problem for the
local authorities to deal with, not the government. Hopkinson
concluded by offering the information that his, and other,
government departments were discussing whether or not to set
up a committee. He did not say what the committee would discuss – a strange silence, given that the only identified problem
was one which he considered to be local authority responsi-
bility.

The main subject of this 1954 debate was immigration control, and those to be controlled were 'coloured colonial immigrants'. This was to become the predominant political definition
of the problem. In 1954, however, that view was held by only
a minority of MPs. Moreoever, other interpretations were
expressed. A group of Labour MPs representing London constituencies organised a debate on housing on 22 November
1957. Their intention was to demonstrate that the arrival of
overseas British subjects in London was highlighting an already
desperate situation. Albert Evans, MP for south-west Islington,
opened the debate by making this very claim and then explicitly
rejecting the definition of the problem in terms of immigration
control. Although he categorised the migrants as a 'race' by
talking about Britain becoming a 'society of many races' and
made references to 'coloured people', this categorisation was
not linked with a demand for immigration control. Indeed,
Evans was very anxious to present the West Indian migrants in
a positive light by stressing the contribution that they made to
the British economy:

> In this connection, I must mention that the good work done
> by the coloured women in our hospitals is deserving of
> favourable comment, and we should thank them for doing

work which, very often, our long-standing citizens would not
readily do.

As far as he was concerned, the problem was the housing shortage. He went on to refer to the activities of property speculators
and to local authorities' inability to deal with overcrowding
because of that shortage. Eric Fletcher, MP for east Islington,
argued that one of the consequences of continued overcrowding
was the expression of racism:

> Overcrowding is causing colour prejudice. Colour prejudice is
> not spontaneous in this country – British people are friendly
> to coloured immigrants – but the degree of prejudice is
> growing as a result of these housing conditions.

B. Parkin, representing north Paddington, went on: 'The problem arises from the need to have accommodation for lower-paid
workers near the centre of London because London needs such
people.'

These three speakers were consistent in their definition of the
problem as the long-term failure to provide sufficient, adequate
housing. But not all their Labour colleagues appreciated this
argument. For example, C.W.Gibson, MP for Clapham, after
stating that the state had a duty to provide adequate accommodation for 'coloured immigrants', went on to call for an agreement between the British government and the governments of
the West Indies voluntarily to limit their entry into Britain.
Marcus Lipton, MP for Brixton, articulated the contradictory
position most succinctly when he argued that the housing problem in London is growing 'because it is bound to grow so long
as immigration into this country continues. It is bound to grow
so long as building by local authorities is restricted.'

Replying for the government J.R.Bevins, Parliamentary
Secretary to the Ministry of Housing and Local Government,
acknowledged the value of West Indian labour:

> We ought to recognise that a large proportion of these people
> coming to London and our provincial cities succeed in finding
> useful work and make a very valuable contribution to the
> nation's economy.

But, as for London's housing shortage, that was simply 'intractable'. Bevins merely promised to give the problem further attention.

This 1957 debate provided an alternative diagnosis of Britain's problem. If British capitalism required more labour than could be effectively supplied from the population then living in Britain, and if British citizens from overseas were prepared to meet the shortfall, then the suppliers of that labour power should be adequately housed. Such had been the argument of the Royal Commission on Population in 1949. The provision of housing is part of the cost of the reproduction of labour power, and where this is not directly undertaken by employers, the duty falls to the state. The Conservative government shifted the onus when it claimed that overcrowding was a local authority problem. But those arguing this position did not directly confront those who identified the problem in terms of the presence of the 'coloured colonial immigrants' and of the need to reduce this presence. By 1958, this latter position had gained ground. It was reiterated by another Labour MP in a debate on 3 April 1958.

On that day, A.Hynd, representing Accrington, moved the following motion:

> That, in the opinion of this House, the time has arrived for
> reconsideration of the arrangements whereby British subjects
> from other parts of the Commonwealth are allowed to enter
> this country without restriction.

Hynd's justification for moving this motion was that the growing number of immigrants were spreading disease, adding to the housing problem, increasing the size of school classes and swelling the demands on National Assistance. Although anxious to point out his opposition to any control on immigration in terms of 'race, colour or creed', he added that without immigration control 'prejudice' would increase. In other words, it was considered necessary to control 'coloured immigration' in order to prevent an increase in 'racial prejudice'.

This call for a racist policy was seconded by Conservative MP for north Devon, James Lindsay. He was more explicit on who should be subject to restriction:

> This is a great influx of coloured people into this country and
> it will make a difference to the composition of the population.

We are starting on the road to becoming a multi-racial
country, a mixed community. We must face the facts . . .
Multi-racial countries have a colour problem, and we must
accept that. We see it in countries like South Africa and
America and in the mixed colonies; and a very deplorable and
sad thing it is.

In other words, the 'colour problem' is best solved by preventing people of 'colour' from coming to Britain. Again, Marcus
Lipton, Labour MP for Brixton, expressed support for both the
speakers and the motion.

On this occasion, it was the Joint Under-Secretary of State
for the Home Department who replied. Patricia Hornsby-Smith
rejected Hynd's claims to know the facts, except to acknowledge that there was a housing problem. However, she conceded
in principle that the presence of 'coloured colonial immigrants'
was potentially problematic; in fact, her department had conducted 'special enquiries' into their involvement in crime and
representation amongst the unemployed. But there were no
enquiries into the extent of racial discrimination. She concluded: 'we remain reluctant to contemplate any departure
from our traditional readiness to receive all citizens who have
the status of a British subject.'

Although the weight of these various contributions to political debate in the House of Commons was on the side of the
'race/immigration' problem construction, they were themselves
peripheral to the main business of the House of Commons.
Many issues are identified as political problems through the
medium of parliamentary questions and adjournment debates
without them becoming the object of wider, national attention.
These debates and questions were not reflected in widespread
media coverage or major speeches outside the House of Commons. They were, however, indicative of the particular formulation of a political problem and its solution.

Mutterings and discontent outside the House

First, we must consider the Conservative Cabinet. Official
government replies to individual MP's questions and motions
supported the principle of unrestricted entry of British citizens.
We now know that this expression of principle was built on

shifting sands. There was a discussion of the 'problem' of New Commonwealth 'immigration' in 1954 in the Cabinet and, in early 1955, a decision was taken to draft legislation to reduce it. Harold Macmillan records in his memoirs that Winston Churchill, whom he had replaced as leader of the Conservative Party, was unhappy about this decision:

> I remember that Churchill rather maliciously observed that
> perhaps the cry of 'Keep Britain White' might be a good
> slogan for the election which we should soon have to fight
> without the benefit of his leadership.

Although no further consideration was given to 'immigration' in the Cabinet before 1958, this was indication enough of how the government would respond to an increase in racist pressure.

Second, there was the civil service. Here, too, 'immigration' was defined as a problem. Some joint departmental committees had been formed and had met, and official investigations of, for example, the degree of West Indians' involvement in crime, were conducted, as was revealed by Patricia Hornsby-Smith. The relationship between this limited civil service activity and the Cabinet will remain unclear until the Cabinet papers for the period are made available, in 1987.

Third, there was the Conservative Party itself. In 1955, the central council of the party passed a resolution calling for legislation which would make Commonwealth citizens subject to the same entry regulations as aliens. At the party conference in the same year, the call for health checks on 'immigrants' was raised in five separate motions. These were not major pressures and other matters received much greater attention, but the fact that these demands were expressed is indicative that the problem was the 'coloured immigrants', rather than the racism that was increasingly evident, for example, in bans on West Indians attending dance halls.

Fourth, there was the labour movement. Within the Labour Party, there was no public expression of the views of those right-wing Labour MPs who were calling for controls over 'coloured colonial immigrants'. Two separate Labour Party sub-committees issued reports in 1955. These defined the problem as one of racial discrimination, opposed any unilateral government action to restrict the entry of Commonwealth citizens, and called for the government to assist the 'integration' of immigrants. At the 1956 Labour Party Conference, a motion expressing opposition to racial discrimination was passed. The same cannot be said for the trade union movement. In the mid-1950s, the general secretaries of the National Union of Railwaymen and the Transport and General Workers' Union both expressed support for immigration control; the General Council of the Trades Union Congress was then forced to confront the issue. It did so against the background of a motion passed at the 1955 conference opposing racial discrimination. But a General Council report to that same conference referred to a meeting with the Minister for Labour, during which TUC representatives had requested the government to introduce controls on immigration – although not based on 'colour'. Having declared its policy in this way, the General Council could simply note, in its 1956 report, the NUR's decision to support immigration control.

The 1958 'riots'

In August and September 1958, there were major disturbances in Nottingham and London. The predominant political reaction to these disturbances, and not their occurrence *per se*, proved a decisive factor in ensuring the pre-eminence of the 'race/immigration' definition of a problem. The events themselves constituted a focus for political debate and conflict, in the course of which various right-wing individuals and forces, some of whom had been active in the early 1950s, were able to push the political debate in their ideological direction. They were aided in this by the fact that the state, particularly in the form of the government, proved itself unwilling to act decisively against them, while voices in the labour movement were actively supporting them.

The disturbances themselves require attention in the light of the way in which they were subsequently interpreted. In Nottingham on 23 August, a fight between a group of West Indian migrants and British-born residents followed an alleged assault on a British-born woman by a West Indian. In this fight, six British-born people were said to have been stabbed, and a large mob then set about attacking any West Indian in sight. On the following two Saturday nights, a similar crowd gathered with the aim of attacking West Indian people and their property. The disturbances in London involved larger crowds and were spread over a wider geographical area, loosely described as Notting Hill. The incidents were most numerous on 23, 30 and 31 August and 1 and 2 September, and took two main forms. They consisted of attacks by British-born residents upon either West Indian people or their property. Overall, in this period, the police arrested 177 people, the majority of whom were British-born. Although West Indians were arrested on breach of the peace and possession of offensive weapons charges, all the sources indicate that their behaviour was a response to provocation. The provocation included mobs chanting 'Down with the Niggers' and carrying banners with the slogan 'Deport all Niggers' as they chased and attacked West Indians.

These slogans, along with the fact that West Indians and West Indian property were the objects of attack, show that racism within the working class was a significant political force. However, this was not the predominant political conclusion that was drawn after the disturbances were stopped. Political and media reaction consistently labelled the disturbances 'race riots', and it was within the ideological framework of 'race' that almost all attempts to explain them occurred. In the immediate aftermath of the attacks on West Indians and their property, four main explanations and solutions were proposed.

The first identified the problem as a lack of respect for 'law and order' on the part of an unrepresentative section of British youth: the solution was to be found in a strict enforcement of the law. The second referred to a lack of mutual understanding and education: it urged an increase in welfare services and a greater willingness on the part of West Indians to 'integrate' into British life (a solution that ignored their attempts to do so by attending dance halls, from which they were banned). A third, rarely heard, yet most accurate, explanation was that the riots were a consequence of 'racial prejudice': its proponents called for action to eliminate discrimination from British society. But it was the fourth, the 'immigration control' response, that carried the day.

The first political responses to the riots were printed in the *Times* on 27 August, under the headline 'Nottingham MPs Urge

Curb on Entry of Immigrants'. Two Nottingham MPs (J.Harrison, Labour MP for Nottingham north, and Lieutenant-Colonel J.K.Cordeaux, Conservative MP for Nottingham central) had criticised the 'open door' policy. The following day, the *Times* continued the same theme. A story headlined 'Renewed Call for Changes in Immigration Law' reported the familiar views of Norman Pannell and Cyril Osborne. Government's response was to admit that it had

> for some time been examining the result of this country's
> time-honoured practice to allow free entry of immigrants
> from Commonwealth and colonial countries. While this study
> of major policy and its implications and effects on
> employment will continue, her Majesty's Government do not
> think it right to take long-term decisions, except after careful
> consideration of the problem as a whole.

This was hardly a statement of principled opposition to the demand for immigration control. Rather, by conceding that it had been considering this option for some time, the government was advertising its willingness to accept the racist case.

Subsequent press reporting continued to emphasise this theme. A group of West Indian politicians flew to Britain to assess for themselves what had happened; their presence was consistently reported in the *Times* in relation to the possibility of immigration controls. The four main stories in the *Times* between 9 and 13 September had the following headlines: 'Frank Talks on Racial Issue: Move to Control Immigration: Voluntary Curb Suggested'; 'Ways to Check Exodus from West Indies Discussed: Plans for Future Outlined at Colonial Office Talks'; 'West Indies Unlikely to Apply Voluntary Limit on Emigrants: Mr Manley Sums up British Tour'; 'W. Indian Guests at No.10: Racial Problems Discussed: Possible Scheme for Expulsions'. In two of these headlines, the link between 'race' and 'immigration' is explicit and in the other two implicit. Hence, not only was the demand for 'immigration control' immediately proposed as the political solution to racist attacks on West Indians, but this demand was used systematically to frame subsequent 'news'. That the attacks were racist was, of course, obscured by the description of the events of 1958 as a 'race riot' or 'colour problem'.

The response of the labour movement was, to say the least, ambiguous. As we have already seen, a Nottingham MP was amongst the first to call for controls over immigration. He received sympathetic support from the Labour MP for Kensington north, Mr Rogers, who blamed the government for failing to introduce legislation to deal with the 'racial problem'. He told the *Times* that the 'immigrants' overcrowded accommodation 'which is needed by white people', and the *Daily Sketch* that:

> The government must introduce legislation quickly to end the
> tremendous influx of coloured people from the
> Commonwealth . . . Overcrowding has fostered vice, drugs,
> prostitution and the use of knives. For years the white people
> have been tolerant. Now their tempers are up.

The leader of the Labour Party, Hugh Gaitskell, responded differently. He denounced hooliganism, claiming that it damaged Britain's national reputation and would 'increase racial tension without in any way solving the underlying social and economic problems'. Later, at the end of September, the Labour Party set out a more detailed policy to meet 'the challenge of racialism' – its main demand was for legislation to make discrimination illegal. Significantly, neither Gaitskell's immediate reaction, nor the later official statement, explicitly confronted those within the labour movement who were calling for controls.

The annual conference of the TUC was in session during the attacks. One delegate argued that they had demonstrated that some workers held racist views; the General Council offered a different interpretation. Its statement made much of the activities of neo-fascist agitation and the need for the 'immigrants' to 'accustom themselves' to a new way of life, while the general secretary claimed in debate:

> I hope that there will never be a wall built round this country
> to keep out people who are entitled to hold the same passport
> as we hold. I would, however, express the personal opinion
> that there should be gates in their land of origin and here
> through which people must pass.

Moreover, in its annual report to Congress, the General Council had referred to discussions with the Minister of Labour in which TUC representatives had called for controls over immigration and the introduction of health checks for immigrants.

The main parliamentary response to the attacks on West Indians came in December 1958 when Cyril Osborne initiated a debate on immigration control. Although he claimed that he desired controls 'irrespective of colour or race', he added that it was useless 'denying that opinion in this country is most exercised by the coloured immigrant'. M.Lindsay, Conservative MP for Solihull, was even more explicit: 'We all know perfectly well that the whole core of the problem of immigration is coloured immigration. We would do much better to face that and to discuss it realistically in the context.' For him, the problem was not 'coloured immigration' *per se*:

> We must ask ourselves to what extent we want Great Britain
> to become a multi-racial community. If that is our desire and
> we decide to make it a matter of deliberate policy, well and
> good, but let us at least consider where we are going and
> make up our minds whether that is what we want, and not
> simply drift . . . A matter which affects the future of our race
> and breed is not one that we should leave merely to chance.

Lindsay clearly wanted to define the issue in the terms employed by the 1949 Royal Commission on Population.

Understanding the 1958 disturbances in terms of 'race/immigration' implied that they had a natural rather than a social origin. The introduction of the idea of 'race' serves to present physical differences between people as an objective determinant of their culture and social behaviour. Once that idea had been used to interpret the riots, the latter came to be viewed as the inevitable outcome of 'race' difference: the riots had demonstrated that Britain too had a 'colour problem'. As it was the West Indian migrants who were consistently described as 'coloured', it followed that it was the West Indian presence in Britain which was problematic. The solution was therefore 'obvious': stop West Indians coming to Britain. The Conservative government was not yet able or willing to 'see' this, and more effort was required to push it firmly on to the slippery slope to state racism.

Down the slippery slope

The attacks on West Indians and their property in 1958 allowed the small group of racists inside and outside parliament to speak to a national audience. This was a significant advance in the racialisation of British politics. Not until the late 1960s were the racists again presented with such a good opportunity to put their case to a national audience, so much of their subsequent agitation was at a regional level or consisted of lobbying within the Conservative Party. The focus for both activities shifted to the English Midlands.

The 1959 general election returned not only a Conservative government, but also a number of new Conservative MPs in the Midlands who soon proved themselves to be supporters of the cause long advocated by Osborne and Pannell. As well as growing in size, this lobby also became more organised. Harold Gurden, Conservative MP for Selly Oak, organised a series of meetings in late 1960 and early 1961 of Back Bench MPs to discuss immigration control and to lobby the Home Secretary.

These developments took on added significance in the light of the formation of the Birmingham Immigration Control Association in October 1960. This small but very active and vociferous association conducted a political campaign in the Midlands: it organised protest meetings, the distribution of leaflets, the collection of signatures on petitions and writing letters to the local press. These activities received widespread attention in the *Birmingham Mail*. The ideological nature of the association's campaign is best illustrated by the comments of one of its leading members, Conservative councillor Charles Collett. Writing about an Indian in a letter published in the *Birmingham Evening Dispatch* (10 November 1959), he claimed:

> He had no fear of starvation, as we should have in his
> country. His friends would soon put him wise to the National
> Assistance Board. What a foolish race we are to tolerate the
> uncontrolled, unhealthy influx of coloured immigrants.

Like Cyril Osborne, BICA was not concerned with immigration *per se*, but with ensuring that Britain was 'a white man's country'. Consequently, the question of 'immigration' was inextricable from 'race'. A crucial interdependence between this association and those Midlands MPs emerged: the latter could cite the association as evidence of 'grassroots' opinion, while the association could attempt to realise its aim through political pressure on the MPs.

This interdependence, and the associated political activity, received national publicity, as did the continuing activities of Osborne, who had won a ballot to present a Private Member's Bill to the House of Commons in February 1961. Although his Bill called for the introduction of immigration control, irrespective of 'race, colour or creed', his real intentions were revealed just 10 days before the debate in the House of Commons when he was quoted in the *Daily Mail* as saying: 'This is a white man's country and I want it to remain so.' He was more reticent in the House of Commons on 17 February, but when questioned about the emphasis in his speech on the increasing size of the 'coloured population', he replied: 'Yes, they obviously present a much greater difficulty. Any Hon. Member who doubts that fact is doing a disservice to this country.' When asked to explain, he answered, 'Because they have altogether a different standard of civilisation to begin with.' Norman Pannell continued the same theme: 'There is a standard of civilisation which is lower and there are acquired habits and inclinations which conflict with the accepted pattern of this country, which has evolved over the centuries.'

Replying for the government, David Renton, Joint Under-Secretary of State for the Home Department, again referred to the principle of maintaining the right of entry of British subjects and asked that the motion be withdrawn. However, the tone had shifted: Renton emphasised that the government was watching the situation with 'care' and 'concern', and agreed with the motion's supporters that the 'immigrants' were exacerbating existing social problems. This is very different from Prime Minister Harold Macmillan's curt reply to a question from Osborne on 24 January 1957: 'I would deprecate any reflection that may be cast on the standards of health and conduct of these immigrants.'

Such national and regional activity, in combination with considerable media attention, was providing a focus for 'public opinion': by 1961 'race/immigration' was well defined as a problem which people should have views about. In addition, the immigration statistics were showing a sharp increase in immigration from the Caribbean and the Indian sub-continent in 1960 and 1961. Research by Ceri Peach clearly demonstrates that this increase was a direct response to the threat of the imposition of control: intending migrants of British citizenship, worried that their right of entry was to be withdrawn, no longer waited for a likely job to be reported by a brother or friend. Rather, they decided to 'beat the ban' and migrate whatever the economic circumstances in Britain. Racist agitation therefore fulfilled its own prophecies: an apparently ever-increasing stream of 'coloured colonial immigrants'. In May 1961, a Gallup Poll reported that 73 per cent of the British population favoured immigration control; in September, at the annual conference of the Conservative Party, there were 39 resolutions in favour of immigration control, compared with 7 in 1960. In the debate, Home Secretary Butler spoke in ambiguous terms; on 31 October, however, the Queen's Speech announced that Her Majesty's Government intended to withdraw the right of entry to Britain of British citizens in the Commonwealth. This was the first major step towards the realisation of Osborne's intention.

The Commonwealth Immigrants Act (1962)

The right of entry was withdrawn from Commonwealth citizens by the Commonwealth Immigrants Act (1962). The Act stated that British citizens living in the Commonwealth could enter Britain only if they possessed a Ministry of Labour employment voucher, or if they were a dependant of such a person already resident in Britain, or a student. There were three categories of voucher. 'Category A' vouchers were to be issued to Commonwealth citizens who had a specific job to come to in Britain. 'Category B' vouchers were to be issued to Commonwealth citizens who had a recognised skill or qualification which was in short supply in Britain. 'Category C' vouchers were available to all other applicants, with priority given to those who had served in the British armed forces during the war. The Act was introduced as a temporary measure and contained the provision that it should be renewed annually.

The Act appeared rational, appeared to have rejected the idea of control based on 'race'. Not only did it apply to all British citizens with passports issued by Commonwealth governments, but it appeared to relate the rate of migration to the availability of jobs in the British economy. Concerning the latter, it is important to recall that neither employers nor their political pressure groups had joined the chorus calling for control. The method of control did not, therefore, prevent capital from recruiting labour from outside Britain, although it could now do so only with the co-operation of the state. These appearances are belied by the evidence.

First, the legislation was introduced primarily as a result of the political campaign to reduce 'coloured colonial immigration' and to ensure that Britain remained a 'white man's country'. That campaign had supporters both within and outside the House of Commons, and had both mobilised public opinion and artificially increased the rate of migration into Britain after 1959. Prior to that date, the flow of migrant labour had corresponded closely with fluctuations in the demand for labour in Britain. Second, if the justification for the legislation was to establish 'rational' control of immigration in order to ensure both a supply of labour and the 'integration' of those who supplied that labour, then the government should also have acted to provide all the facilities – including housing and education – required for this addition to the workforce. The fact that it had not done so, and did not do so, suggests that the government was motivated primarily by the negative intention of preventing the entry of a particular group of people, 'coloured people'. Third, the Act did not apply to the entry of citizens of the Irish Republic, who were not even British citizens. Yet, as the Home Secretary admitted when opening the debate on the second reading of the Bill on 16 November 1961, some 60,000 to 70,000 citizens of the Irish Republic were then entering Britain annually. That the Act did not regulate this flow of migrant labour demonstrates its real aim: to obstruct the entry of one particular group of migrants, 'coloured' migrants. In sum, the government's legislation embodied the very requirement set out by the 1949 Royal Commission on Population, to meet the demand for labour by migrants considered to be 'of good stock' – read 'white'.

The Labour Party opposed and voted against the Bill in both

its second and third readings. Its opposition was founded on both political and economic grounds. Concerning the former, Hugh Gaitskell, Leader of the Labour Party, said on 16 November: 'It is a plain anti-Commonwealth measure in theory and it is a plain anti-colour measure in practice.' Most Labour MPs who spoke in the debate defended the right of free entry for Commonwealth citizens and attacked the Conservative Party for having rejected the Commonwealth and the principles on which it was founded. They also consistently accused the government of implementing racism. As Gordon Walker, Labour MP for Smethwick, said of the Home Secretary on 16 November: 'He advocates a Bill into which race discrimination is now written – not only into its spirit and its practice, but into its very letter.'

The Labour Party's economic case was premised on the fact that the flow of migration from the New Commonwealth up until 1959 had been regulated by the demand for labour in the British economy. It followed that there were no grounds for state regulation of entry. Moreover, although the political aim was defined as the need to reduce immigration, the legislation ensured that any expansion in the economy could and would still lead to an increase in migration. In this connection, a comparison was drawn with the large migration flows into other European countries and their continuing economic growth (see chapter 6). Furthermore, they argued that the Bill could not justifiably be considered to deal with the economic and social problems which the government claimed to be a consequence of too high a level of migration. Again with reference to the Bill's provision concerning the citizens of the Republic of Ireland, James MacColl, MP for Widnes, argued:

> To try to pretend that the Bill is needed to tackle grave social problems by stopping people coming over regardless of the rules by making them obtain job vouchers, while excluding from it the main group of people involved who come here and use our services, makes the whole thing complete nonsense.

The case against the Bill made by the Labour Party was, in the main, based on principle and firm evidence even though, as Hugh Gaitskell conceded on 16 November, the party's opposition may have been contrary to public opinion, 'but, even if this were the case, I do not believe it to be our duty merely to follow what we are convinced are wrong and dangerous views.'

Yet, there remained a crucial correspondence between the two political parties. They agreed that the migrant workers from the New Commonwealth were of a different 'race', although the Labour Party then argued that the history of colonialism placed certain responsibilities upon the 'white race'. As Gordon Walker put it in the debate on the second reading:

> although relationships between people of the white race and
> other races is a world-wide problem, it is, in a special sense,
> a peculiar Commonwealth problem. European imperialism
> imposed a long period of domination by whites over peoples
> of other colours.

Moreover, when Denis Healey, MP for east Leeds, summed up the Labour case at the end of the third reading, he hedged on a direct question about what the Labour Party would do if elected to govern:

> If the information collected by a serious survey of the whole
> problem revealed that immigration control was necessary, we
> should regard it as essential to consult the other
> Commonwealth Governments . . . We would consult other
> Commonwealth Governments to see how this could be
> achieved with the minimum damage to their interests and to
> their confidence in our loyalty and good will. This is how we
> shall act when we win power.

Clearly, underneath the commitment to principle there existed all the elements of the 'race/immigration' construction of the problem, a construction that had been expressed in the labour movement as early as 1954.

Conclusion

By 1962, the presence of migrant labour from the Caribbean and the Indian sub-continent had been made the object of major political debate in Britain. The labour power of these migrants was eagerly sought by capitalists and sections of the state, but a small group of politicians and political activists

objected and conducted a hostile campaign against their presence. Moreover, because the state made no additional provision for this increase in the semi- and unskilled labour force
(the housing shortage remained and no new resources were
made available for education and social welfare), the material
conditions existed for a hostile response from those sections of
the working class which the migrants joined. The hostility of
both politicians and sections of the working class focused upon
certain physical characteristics of the migrants, notably their
skin colour, and came to be expressed in terms of the idea of
'race'. In this way, a notion of difference between the migrants
and the indigenous population was politically constructed, one
which conceived of each as a biologically distinct group, a different 'race'. Additionally, 'they' were attributed with a
number of further characteristics, each negatively evaluated;
'they' had a propensity to crime, created slums or, more
broadly, represented a 'lower level of civilisation'.

This ideological interpretation emerged from an ideological
struggle. The arrival of the migrants was understood in different
ways, as was evident throughout the late 1950s and in the political debate over the Commonwealth Immigrants Bill. The
decision of the Conservative government to legislate to control
the entry of 'coloured colonial immigrants' was an endorsement
of the arguments put forward by a small group of racist politicians and activists. By so doing, the government confirmed the
apparent reality of 'race': physical characteristics became a criterion of entry into Britain for people who were British citizens
by virtue of their Commonwealth status. As William Deedes, a
government minister at the time, recalled in 1968: 'The Bill's
real purpose was to restrict the influx of coloured immigrants.
We were reluctant to say as much openly.' British politics were
racialised at the highest level; state racism became a reality.

3. The institutionalisation of state racism, 1962–71

Introduction

There were many in the Conservative Party, including most of the leadership, who hoped and believed that the passage of the 1962 Act was the end of the matter. But, for the right wing, the vision of Britain as a 'white man's country' was still a long way from being realised. 'Immigration' (that is, the entry of 'coloured people') had not been stopped, and there was the prospect of those 'immigrants' already resident raising a new generation of 'coloured people' born in Britain. In fact, the 1962 Act encouraged the latter. By restricting entry, it forced those migrants who might have returned to the Caribbean or the Indian sub-continent periodically to visit their families while working as migrants in Britain, to settle and raise a family in Britain. The fear of not being able to return to Britain, along with the continuing demand for their labour, turned the majority of migrant workers into settlers – people who would remain in Britain, and retain just the hope of return.

This was reflected in the post-1962 immigration statistics which soon showed an increase in the number of people entering Britain from the New Commonwealth as dependants of people already resident. Table 3.1 shows this by distinguishing between New Commonwealth migrants entering Britain as voucher holders and those entering as dependants between mid-1962 and 1967. Only in the case of migrants from the Indian sub-continent in 1963 did the number of voucher-holding entrants exceed the number of arrivals of dependants. As the Conservative government had justified its racist legislation by arguing that it wanted to reduce the number of immigrants entering Britain, it was possible for the right wing to pursue their vision by simply pointing out that, on this criterion, the Act was failing.

Thus, once 'immigration control' had been successfully estab-

Table 3.1 Commonwealth citizens arriving in the UK from the Caribbean and Indian sub-continent, July 1962–December 1967

| | Indian sub-continent | | Caribbean | |
	voucher holders	dependants	voucher holders	dependants
1962*	1,037	2,070	1,600	3,730
1963	21,892	9,920	2,077	7,896
1964	7,124	15,816	2,635	11,461
1965	6,314	19,561	2,987	11,147
1966	3,154	22,676	628	878
1967	2,929	33,328	630	11,211

* July–December
Source Commonwealth Immigrants Act (1962) statistics

lished under the political spotlight as the problem, racists could continue to press their case without necessarily mentioning 'race' or 'inferior stock': their earlier agitation had now established in common-sense thought that an immigrant was, by definition, 'coloured'. What they had to ignore was that the flow of migrant labour into Britain continued – not from the Commonwealth, but from Ireland and from other European countries outside the European Economic Community (see Table 3.2). This ensured that employers (including the state) had no reason to formulate an economic case against the racist Commonwealth Immigrants Act, and left the racists a political arena free from economic considerations to continue their campaign. Their political and ideological autonomy was therefore considerable. Their main opposition appeared to be the Labour Party because, despite its prevarications on the question of the abolition of the 1962 Act, it had nevertheless made a principle of its opposition to racism and racial discrimination. When it failed to honour this principle, the way was clear for the full institutionalisation of racism in the practice of the state.

Racism and the Labour Party

The expression of racism had not been limited to the right wing of the Conservative Party and the tiny neo-fascist groups (see chapter 5 on the latter). It was also being expressed in the pubs, factories and council estates, as sections of the working class struggled with the realities of a shortage of adequate housing, limited educational facilities for their children and the general

Table 3.2 Migrant workers entering Britain under voucher and work permit schemes, 1965–70

	Commonwealth workers with voucher	Foreign workers (non-EEC) with work permit
1965	16,046	54,258
1966	8,300	54,837
1967	8,409	50,303
1968	8,120	51,476
1969	6,769	56,156
1970	5,563	56,006

Source Racism, Who Profits?, CIS Report

physical decline of working-class areas. West Indian workers were excluded from trade and labour clubs and there was industrial action when New Commonwealth workers were employed or promoted in factories in various parts of Britain. It was the reality of this racism that formed the substance of the following taunt of John Harvey, Conservative MP for Walthamstow east, directed towards the Labour Party in the debate on the third reading of the Commonwealth Immigrants Bill:

> it is surely fair to point out that there has been the case of a
> trade and labour club which decided to ban coloured
> members. Many Hon. Members opposite were, quite rightly,
> concerned about that. It would also be fair to point out in this
> context that there have been strikes by trade unionists against
> this employment of coloured labour. In this context, too, it
> would be fair to point out that some of the areas in which
> racial strife has broken out are certainly not areas in which
> the Conservative Party flourishes.

It was easier for the Labour Party to respond to such taunts than to deal with the expression of racism within the ranks of the labour movement – especially when the party had shown a willingness to compromise principle for what it saw as electoral advantage. The reasons are clear from what happened in the constituency of Smethwick, Birmingham, in the 1950s and 1960s.

In 1950, Gordon Walker was elected Labour MP for this constituency and immediately became Secretary of State for Commonwealth Relations. He was therefore a politician of some significance. On 12 November 1954, he joined that small number of labour movement members who were advocating control over Commonwealth immigration. In March 1955, he responded thus to a Smethwick landlord's introduction of a 'whites only' rule to the already sexist institution of the 'men only' smoking-room: 'I can see nothing to be gained by changing the well-established law of this country which leaves the question of licensing to the local licensing justices.' This was hardly a forthright condemnation of racism within his constituency. Yet Gordon Walker rose in the House of Commons, on 16 November 1961, to put the Labour Party's case against the Commonwealth Immigrants Bill. It was an act that caused considerable hostility towards him in Smethwick, as is evident in the letter-pages of the local paper, the *Smethwick Telephone*. He should not have been surprised.

From 1960, a series of racist letters had appeared in the local paper. A letter published on 22 July 1960, written by a Mr Rieper, included the following declaration:

> It is tragic, indeed, to see a fine race destroyed by blood
> poisoning. These coloured people are bribed to come here by
> doles, National Assistance and all the amenities of the
> Welfare State free. Our racial future is at stake.

This letter-campaign presaged the formation of a branch of the Birmingham Immigration Control Association (BICA) on 24 March 1961 – at a meeting attended by senior members of Smethwick Labour Party. The committee of the Smethwick branch of the BICA contained a majority of working-class people who had voted Labour for most of their lives. Four public meetings were organised in the spring and early summer, all of which were attended by over 200 people. In July 1961, the largest youth club in Smethwick announced that it was excluding 'coloured youth'. The president of the club was a former Labour councillor. These various events indicated the existence of a 'spontaneous' grassroots protest movement and the organisation of public opinion in the area around the ideological notion of the 'race/immigration' problem. Those active in this organisation of opinion faced no opposition from their MP.

In March 1962, Mr Finney, chairman of the BICA branch in Smethwick, dissolved the branch, promptly joined the Conservative Party and was adopted as a candidate for the municipal elections. Having been elected, he campaigned with the leader of the Conservatives on the local council, Peter Griffiths (who was also the prospective parliamentary candidate), on an 'anti-immigration' platform. Their campaign continued up to and throughout the general election of 1964. When Gordon Walker complained that, during the municipal elections in May 1963, children had been organised to chant 'If you want a nigger neighbour, vote Labour,' Peter Griffiths commented to the *Times*: 'I would not condemn anyone who said that. I regard it as a manifestation of popular feeling.' Griffiths's endorsement of racism was thus publicly coupled with his loud and regular calls for 'immigration control'.

Although Gordon Walker was largely silent in his constituency, he had more to say in the Shadow Cabinet. He argued that the Labour Party should not oppose the renewal of the Commonwealth Immigrants Act when it came before the House of Commons in November 1963, and cited the need to respond to public 'fears' and opinion. No doubt, public opinion was exemplified in Gordon Walker's mind by the slogan 'If you want a nigger neighbour, vote Labour.' The Shadow Cabinet finally compromised between those supporting the Gordon Walker position and those rejecting renewal on the same grounds as the Bill had been opposed. The new leader of the Labour Opposition, Harold Wilson, announced to the House of Commons on 27 November:

> Those three grounds which were the grounds of our
> opposition to the Bill are just as true today as they were
> then . . . I come to the general issue about the control of
> immigration. We do not contest the need for control of
> immigration into this country.

Wilson went on to call for an alternative means of controlling immigration from the Commonwealth; he made no reference to controls over immigration from the Republic of Ireland. He also called for a policy of 'assimilation' of immigrants already in Britain, including legislation against racial discrimination. Thus, for the leadership of the Labour Party in parliament, the political issue was no longer that of a housing shortage – it was immigration control. For the right in the Conservative Party, Pannell pointed out that the Act had led to an increase in immigration and Osborne renewed his predictions of doom:

> The problem is there the world over, and so far no one has
> found a solution to it, and it seems to me the height of folly
> to bring the problem unnecessarily into our midst. It is a
> tragedy for which our children will curse us.

The Act had done little to prevent the 'racial Apocalypse'.
The leadership of the Labour Party, while not sharing this
vision of Armageddon, now accepted control over the entry of
British Commonwealth citizens (but not over citizens of the
Irish Republic).

In Smethwick, Gordon Walker had to deal with Peter Griffiths in the general election campaign of 1964. Griffiths was
preoccupied with just one thing – 'immigration' – and Gordon
Walker was forced to respond. He argued that the Labour Party
was in favour of immigration control and that the vast bulk of
immigration had occurred under a Conservative government.
The implication was that if the Labour Party had been in power
in the 1950s, it would have acted to prevent the 'coloured colonial immigrants' from coming to Britain. This defence simply
compounded the contradictions: it was certainly consistent with
Gordon Walker's position in 1954, but not with his attack on
the Commonwealth Immigrants Bill. In the election, Griffiths
defeated Gordon Walker with a swing to the Conservative
Party of 7.2 per cent; in Britain as a whole, the Labour Party
was elected to govern with a swing in its favour of 3.5 per cent.

In the context of the 1964 general election, the Smethwick
result was quite untypical; nevertheless, it was highly significant
insofar as it demonstrated that the expression of racism was a
vote catcher. This was noted not only by those whose political
goal was to ensure that Britain remained a 'white man's
country', but also by those in both the Labour and Conservative
parties whose goal was to ensure electoral success. For the
labour movement, it was significant for a different reason.

The situation in Smethwick demonstrated that the Labour
Party was deeply compromised on the question of racism.
There is no doubt that opposition to the presence of 'coloured
colonial immigrants' was common amongst the working class
and could be mobilised for electoral purposes, as well as to sustain industrial action. The Smethwick result proved that this
racism could no longer be ignored. An adequate response
depended upon the Labour Party having an adequate under-

standing of why and how racism had become an important component of working-class political consciousness.

This was the outcome of a combination of historical and situation factors. The historical dimension centres on the fact that English/British national consciousness has been shaped by an interpretation of history which placed great emphasis upon colonial glory and the imperial domination over the 'inferior races'. This interpretation has been (and remains) the content of school history lessons and many editorial columns, as well as television and radio programmes. But this, by itself, is less than half the story. We must also consider how the situation in which these received ideas could help make sense of the current 'realities'. There are two aspects to this.

On the one hand, there was the fact of material deprivation amongst the working class. Large numbers of working-class people, although no longer facing long-term unemployment, nevertheless had to cope with a shortage of adequate housing and inferior educational provision for their children. Moreover, these problems were encountered by many in a decaying urban context. When such sections of the working class found that they were being joined in this environment by migrant workers from the New Commonwealth, the potential was there for them to conclude that these migrants would make it more difficult to escape these conditions, if not that the migrants had actually helped create them. That many did come to such conclusions was not simply the consequence of media or political manipulation. It was an 'obvious' common-sense conclusion. It was one which was particularly easy to draw when you 'knew' that migrants were a 'race apart', a different and inferior sort of human being, perhaps even 'animals'; it 'made sense' to conclude that you would not have had to put up with a shared toilet on the stair, damp walls and new neighbours if there was immigration control to keep the 'coloureds' out.

On the other hand, whether or not this conclusion was being drawn 'spontaneously', it was certainly being argued politically from the mid-1950s. For some, this constituted a confirmation of what they had themselves concluded, while for others it was an interpretation of their world which suddenly 'made sense'. Amongst those not directly affected by such problems, the common-sense logic of the argument could have an appeal in the absence of information and/or a political perspective which pointed to quite different conclusions. There was, therefore, a complex interaction between grassroots political consciousness and formal political activity and propaganda, mediated by the sort of newspaper and television coverage that we discussed in chapter 1.

As a consequence of these complex interactions, the idea of 'race' and the problem of immigration were combined and came to the fore in working-class political consciousness. They became the subject of conversation in the factory, the shops and the pub. This was not some automatic reflex, a direct product of historical tradition. Without material and social disadvantage, these ideas would have had much less appeal to far fewer people. The failure of governments to house and educate adequately is thus part of the explanation for working-class racism. The Conservative government's failure in the 1950s in this connection was nothing unusual. It is a historical fact that, under capitalism, poverty, bad housing and inadequate social and educational provision have dominated the lives of large sections of the working class: this, too, was (and is) a major condition for the reproduction of racism.

If this is the explanation for working-class expression of racism, it is an explanation that implicates the Labour Party. Although the official policy of the Labour Party was certainly anti-racist, within its ranks other forces and arguments were active. The previous chapter has shown that some prominent individuals in the labour movement played a role in justifying and expressing racism in the 1950s. Moreover, those who were committed to the anti-racist position did not explicitly or consistently challenge the activities and arguments of those proponents of the 'race/immigration' interpretation. The racist interpretation, through lack of challenge, was allowed to fester. The 1964 general election ensured that the Labour Party would have to deal with the consequences.

Labour in power: racism rules OK

One of the earliest decisions facing the new Labour government was whether or not to renew the Commonweath Immigrants Act. In November 1964, the government renewed the Act, but promised to conduct discussions with Commonwealth governments about immigration. Whatever firmly grounded suspicions there might then have been about the government's intentions and motivations, it was at least possible that the racist basis of immigration control would be removed. The first real indication of what was to follow came in February 1965. The Home Secretary reported to the House of Commons that he believed there was considerable evasion of the controls established by the 1962 Act and that he had urged immigration officers to make greater use of their powers. The 'illegal immigrants' scare had begun – initiated by the Labour government. In August 1965, the government published an aptly described White Paper, entitled 'Immigration from the Commonwealth' (Cmnd. 2739). This set out proposals for the strengthening of the 1962 Act when it came up for renewal in November 1965. The White Paper emphasised the large increase in the number of dependants from the New Commonwealth entering Britain since 1963, and described the net total of immigrants from the New Commonwealth as exceeding that from Australia, New Zealand and Canada. This was a coded way of saying that there were more 'coloured colonial immigrants' than 'white colonial immigrants' coming into Britain. There was no mention of the 30,000 citizens of the Irish Republic who would enter Britain in 1965 alone. The Act, condemned in principle as racist in 1962, was now being endorsed and made more effective by the Labour Party in government.

The proposals included the abolition of 'Category C' vouchers, a reduction in the rate of issue of the remaining vouchers to 8,500 a year (of which 1,000 were reserved for citizens of Malta), a strengthening of the powers of deportation, the introduction of health checks and an increase in the powers of immigration officers (including the authority to require a Commonwealth immigrant to register with the police). These proposals, and the subsequent renewal of the Act, constituted a complete endorsement of the 'race/immigration' interpretation of the issues raised by labour migration from the New Commonwealth. The central division between the two main political parties was not whether the 'coloureds' should be kept out, but over how few should be allowed in. The institutionalisation of racism in the area of immigration control was almost complete: now the 'numbers game' could begin in earnest.

The White Paper also defined a new object of political concern and initiative – 'integration'. As a prelude to setting out a programme to ensure integration, the document identified Britain as a 'multi-racial' society, one whose economy required the presence of Commonwealth immigrants. It continued:

> At the same time it must be recognised that the presence in this country of nearly one million immigrants from the Commonwealth with different social and cultural backgrounds raises a number of problems and creates various social tensions in those areas where they have concentrated. If we are to avoid the evil of racial strife and if harmonious ralations between the races who now form our community are to develop, these problems and tensions must be resolved and removed.

This was the first, official statement which defined immigration as leading to a problem of 'race relations'. It also explicitly identified the presence of the immigrants as the origin of the 'race relations' problem. This was confirmed by the fact that the proposals in the White Paper were all concerned with what needed doing for or to 'them'. Again, 'they' were made the object of political attention and the idea of 'race' was given new meaning as a domestic problem requiring local and national government attention. Integration, therefore, meant doing things for, and as a consequence of, the 'coloured' presence.

The debate on the White Paper in the House of Commons on 23 November was bitter. The government had to endure several hours of attack from anti-racist Labour MPs and from Conservative MPs over what they saw as the weakness of the new restrictions. Paul Rose, Labour MP for Blackley, Manchester, spoke for most of the other Labour contributors when he declared: 'this debate is not about the control of immigration, but about colour prejudice and discrimination against coloured Commonwealth citizens.' This view was confirmed by what was said from both the Front and the Back Benches on the Conservative side. Peter Thorneycroft, Conservative spokesman on 'race and immigration' (the fact that such a spokesman existed testifies to the political significance attributed to this ideological construction), referred to the statistical distinction in the White Paper between immigrants from Canada, Australia and New Zealand, and immigrants from other Commonwealth countries:

> But in discussing the matter, if we are going to be honest with ourselves, the question of colour does come in and it is better not to put it under the carpet. We should be quite open about it. There is no other reason why the Home Secretary has drawn the distinction between the two.

John Farr, MP for Harborough, was not alone in wanting restrictions on the number of dependants entering Britain and government support for voluntary 'repatriation'. There was no doubt in his mind about the particular immigrants concerned: 'I merely refer to the fact that this legislation, of which we are considering the renewal, concerns coloured immigrants and what is the point of trying to hide the issue? Why not admit it?' For Henry Brooke, Conservative MP for Hampstead, controls over the entry of 'coloured immigrants' were essential if Britain was to avoid the American experience:

> What we are debating this evening is nothing less than whether we shall be able in this country to avoid the atmosphere of racial bitterness and outbreaks of racial hatred which hang like a menacing cloud permanently over America . . . It is to guard against the possibilities of race tension and race hatred in the future that I am concerned.

Norman St John-Stevas, MP for Chelmsford, and the only Conservative critic of the government who shared some of the concerns of the Labour Back Benchers, defined the problem of immigration as being also a problem of the 'coloured' presence. At the same time, he revealed most clearly of all speakers that night the complete failure of the majority of MPs to acknowledge the facts. He persisted in referring to 'ghettos' after being offered statistical evidence to the contrary by Labour MP Reg Freeson:

> but certainly I think, without relying on statistics, from one's personal experience of visiting areas of immigration, one sees whole streets, roads and areas entirely occupied by coloured people – in North Kensington, for example.

What mattered was not the factual evidence, just personal

experience and emotion. It was on this basis that British politics were racialised.

Labour MPs' criticisms focused on the retreat from principle and on the failure of the government to justify, either politically or with any evidence, the proposals in the White Paper. Their worst suspicions were proved when they heard Ray Gunter, Minister for Labour, refer to instances of industrial action against the promotion of 'coloured workers' to supervisory positions:

> There are industrial tensions, and what we have to consider is
> how much we can contend with prejudice in industry itself. I
> would like to see it disappear overnight, but we know that it
> will not. However, it is a reasonable proposition that we
> should only have, on the numerical strength that we can
> contain.

In reply to the question about why officials in Labour Exchanges marked employment cards with the initials 'CW' (for 'Coloured Worker'), Gunter replied:

> They do it from a sense of Christian charity, because they
> know that if they send a man to a works he will be humiliated,
> often not because the management wants to humiliate him
> but because the management knows that the men on the
> workshop floor will not accept him.

Moreover, 'Whatever may have been said in the House tonight, the country is, in many cases, bursting at the seams.' There were no ambiguities in this speech – just emotional hysteria and an endorsement of working-class racism which took the form of a policy of keeping the 'coloureds' out.

Labour's capitulation was not only in response to racism on the shopfloor. It was also a reaction to continuing agitation within the Conservative Party. In the immediate post-election period, a number of MPs, including the leader of the parliamentary party, demanded new controls to reduce the number of dependants entering Britain. And, in February 1965, Cyril Osborne made it known that he intended to introduce a Bill to stop all immigration except for people whose parents or grandparents had been born in Britain (we shall return to this racist device later). He responded to the pressure of his own Front Bench to modify the Bill, but retained his demand for a policy of assisted, voluntary 'repatriation'. The Bill was defeated on 2 March 1965, but only after Osborne had led a large number of Conservative MPs through the lobby in support of his policy – including Margaret Thatcher, MP. Just four days later, Peter Thorneycroft put forward a series of proposals at the Conservative Party Central Council, including the demand for voluntary 'repatriation'. Patrick Wall, MP, supported these proposals in terms which contained a thinly veiled reference to a 'keep Britain white' policy: 'We must reject the "multi-racial state" not because we are superior to "our Commonwealth Partners", but because we want to maintain the kind of Britain we know and love.'

The Labour government's legitimation of racism was eventually concealed behind a new philosophy. Roy Hattersley, Labour MP for Sparkbrook, Birmingham, put it this way early in 1965: 'Without integration, limitation is inexcusable; without limitation, integration is impossible.' Given the reason for the government's capitulation, Hattersley's clever syllogism was really arguing that in order to eliminate racism within Britain, it is necessary to practise it at the point of entry into Britain. But the Labour government's commitment to 'limitation' was rather stronger than its commitment to 'integration'. The main legislative initiative on the latter was the Race Relations Act (1965), which made racial discrimination illegal and introduced a new offence, 'incitement to racial hatred'. In the interest of gaining Conservative Party support for the legislation, the original Bill was much weakened, but the Labour government alone was responsible for the fact that it did not apply to the areas of employment and housing. Thus, after 1965, it was illegal to discriminate against a West Indian wishing to enter a dance hall, but not illegal to discriminate against the same person when he or she applied for a job.

The political and ideological significance of this legislative support for 'integration' was contradictory. On the one hand, the Race Relations Act (1965) did clearly signal that racial discrimination was a reality and needed to be eliminated. But, on the other, there were several reasons why the Act was inappropriate and had negative consequences. First, as already observed, it did not apply to large areas of economic and social life. Second, its enforcement procedures were weak and lacked the endorsement of a court of law. Third, although there was every reason to redefine the issue of 'integration' away from the supposed problems created by the 'immigrant presence', there was little ideological preparation for this shift in focus and political remedy. Moreover, the fact that racial discrimination was practised by the state at the point of entry into Britain ensured that there was only limited scope for the Act to be taken seriously. Fourth, the focus and title of the legislation ('Race Relations') retained the idea of biologically discrete populations and suggested that their inter-relationship required legal intervention in order to regulate the problems that their contact 'naturally' produced. In reality, racism and discrimination were (and are) concentrated within the indigenous population. Indeed, it was for this very reason that British politics had been racialised.

By legislating *for* 'race relations' instead of *against* racism, the government was giving further substance to the idea of 'race', ensuring that the problem was defined in terms of 'colour', in terms of 'them'. Although the political intention may have been correct, the ideological content of its implementation orginated in and reinforced the 'race/immigration' definition of the problem. The Race Relations Act (1965) was therefore a further phase in the racialisation of British politics, and a complete failure insofar as it was intended to eliminate racial discrimination.

State racism reinforced

By late 1966, both main political parties had lost interest in drawing attention to the 'race/immigration' problem. Certainly, the 1966 general election had not been conducted on the model of Smethwick. There was broad agreement between the two Front Benches about the need to reduce the number of 'coloured colonial immigrants' entering Britain and so the re-elected Labour government began to turn its mind to strengthening the ineffective Race Relations Act (1965). However, a small number of Conservative Back Benchers continued their agitation, and in such a way as to reveal their real, rather than spoken, intentions.

On 21 December 1967, Patrick Wall, MP for Haltemprice, complained to the House of Commons that there was a large outflow of population from Britain to Australia, New Zealand and Canada which was being replaced by people from the New Commonwealth. The latter did not share with the British population the same culture, language and educational background. He was also concerned about the large number of dependants. He continued: 'The nub of the case that I am putting is that many Australians, Canadians and New Zealanders think of themselves as British. They still think about returning to the mother country.' Wall was worried that they were prevented from doing so by the Commonwealth Immigrants Act (1962). But the interest of this group of MPs was not only in cultural difference. Wall had previously rejected the 'multi-racial' state, while in this debate Bernard Braine, Conservative MP for south-east Essex, enquired of the Under-Secretary of State for the Home Department: 'Does the Hon. Gentleman altogether dismiss the fact that Britons, Australians and New Zealanders are people of one blood and bone?'

Hence, as soon as the intending migrants were reputedly people of the same 'blood and bone', there was no longer a problem of numbers, of the country 'bursting at the seams'. It had not mattered to Cyril Osborne and his supporters in the 1950s that West Indian migrants thought of themselves as British and as returning to the 'mother country'. Altogether, it was a way of saying that they wanted Britain to be a 'white man's country'.

At the same time as this debate was taking place, events in East Africa meant that they, and many others, could express this vision in an even more conducive political and ideological atmosphere. The background to these events is discussed in chapter 6. What is significant here is that by the end of 1967, it was clear that there had been an increase in the number of people arriving in Britain from Kenya, people who were in the possession of UK passports, issued by a British High Commission. Because they held a UK passport which was identical to that issued to people born in Britain, they were exempt from the conditions of the Commonwealth Immigrants Act (1962). These people were of Indian origin. On 18 October 1967, Enoch Powell, MP, had referred to these people in a speech made in Deal, saying that a 'loophole' in the 1962 Act allowed a quarter of a million people to belong 'to this country . . . just like you and me'. He returned to the same theme in a speech in Walsall, on 9 February 1968, which was concerned with 'the continued flow of immigration into our towns':

> Some problems are unavoidable. Some evils can be coped with to a certain extent, but not prevented. But that a nation should have saddled itself, without necessity and without countervailing benefit, with a wholly avoidable problem of immense dimensions is enough to make one weep. That the same nation should stubbornly persist in allowing the problem, great as it already is, to be magnified further, is enough to drive one to despair.

Powell's concerns were repeated by Cyril Osborne and Duncan Sandys, and expressed with even less subtlety by the mass media, where the language of an 'uncontrolled flood' and a 'deluge of immigrants' was dominant. To these stories was added, in January 1968, a series of reports about illegal immigrants from Pakistan. That the Kenyan Asians were UK passport holders and British citizens was irrelevant: they were simply perceived as another phase in the 'uncontrolled flood' of 'coloureds', desperate to gain access to the 'honeypot'. Their legitimate and legal entry into Britain was therefore framed by the 'race/immigration' ideology. Consequently, the political hysteria referred primarily to the 95,000 Kenyan Asians holding or entitled to hold UK passports, and not to the total population of the Republic of Ireland which also had the right to enter and work in Britain, but did not hold UK passports, let alone British citizenship.

In the middle of February, the Conservative Shadow Cabinet, of which Powell was a member, called for a tightening of the existing immigration controls and for the provision of financial help for those migrants wishing to return 'home'. On 22 February, the Labour Home Secretary announced to the House of Commons a new Commonwealth Immigrants Bill whose main provision was borrowed from Cyril Osborne's Private Member's Bill of February 1965. The new Bill removed the right of entry into Britain from all British passport holders who did not have a parent or grandparent born in Britain. But, as a 'humanitarian' gesture, those British citizens denied the right of entry were to be allowed to apply for a special voucher which would allow them entry; 1,500 would be issued annually to heads of households. The Bill became law on 1 March.

The Commonwealth Immigrants Act (1968) was even more explicitly racist than its predecessor. It had been introduced as a response to another political campaign initiated by the right-wing of the Conservative Party which mobilised and focused public opinion around the 'race/immigration' theme again. It was an explicit response to the entry of 'coloured' UK passport holders whose right to enter Britain was then withdrawn. None of those involved in the agitation or the passage of the Bill through parliament was concerned about the entry into a Britain which was supposedly 'bursting at the seams' of UK passport holders with a parent or grandparent born in Britain. Such people, of course, were, except in the most anomolous circumstances, 'white'.

The debate on the Bill in the House of Commons indicated how far parliament was prepared to go in legitimating the racism of the British population and institutionalising it in the practice of the state. Labour ministers and Opposition leaders were exceptionally sensitive to this charge and repeatedly denied it. The former added that the Bill was part of a 'race relations' package which would include a new Race Relations Bill later in the year. Much time was taken up over whether or not the 1962 Act contained a 'loophole' through which the Kenyan Asians were 'pouring' or whether there had been a commitment of principle. Although there was hostility and opposition to the Bill, it was limited and muted in comparison to that aroused by the 1965 White Paper – at least on the Labour benches – although the activities of Duncan Sandys and Enoch Powell did excite some invective. Matters of principle were best expressed by Liberal MPs, but there were also vociferous complaints from a number of Conservative MPs who strongly objected to the devaluation of the British passport and who thought that the quota of 1,500 was too low.

The debate on the second and third readings of the Bill, on 27 and 28 February, clearly revealed the almost complete predominance of the 'race/immigration' definition of the problem. When Roland Moyle, Labour MP for north Lewisham, spoke about the inevitability of 'race' tensions arising from the meeting of people of different 'races', Mr Gurden, veteran of the campaign to introduce the 1962 Act, intervened to say: 'I agree with what the Hon. Gentleman says, but, on the point about emigration, it means that a large number of our own flesh and blood are moving out, while we are taking in others from out-side.' Lieutenant-Commander S.L.C.Maydon, Conservative MP for Wells, spelt out the implications for those who believed in the reality of 'races':

> Continuing quotas of people not of British extraction, from wherever they may come, are altering the nature of our race and creating centres . . . where people who are not the same as the rest of us in colour, in racial origin and sometimes in religion hang together . . . I am really scared that unless the Government puts a final stop to immigration of even moderate numbers of people of races different from our own we shall be faced with a situation as bad as that which obtains during the hot summers of New York, Chicago and, more recently, in Detroit.

When Cyril Osborne and Norman Pannell made somewhat milder claims in the House of Commons in the 1950s, they often had difficulty making themselves heard against the hostile reac-tion. Just a decade later, Maydon could be much more explicit and be heard through to the end. Even for those Conservatives of a more 'liberal' persuasion, the problem was explicitly defined as being the 'coloured immigrants' with their 'alien cul-tures'. Reginald Maudling, Conservative MP for Barnet and an ex-government minister, claimed:

> The problem arises quite simply from the arrival in this country of many people of wholly alien cultures, habits and outlook; people incidently, as well, who tend to concentrate in their own communities.

Of even greater significance was the argument that the government was right to respond to 'public opinion'. Frederic Bennett, Conservative Party MP for Torquay, said he was unhappy about the fact that the Bill put in question the commit-ment of politicians to 'non-racialism'. Nevertheless, he was will-ing to accept the argument that

> as MPs in a genuine democracy we have a duty as elected

representatives not deliberately because of our own particular feelings to create a society contrary to the wishes of the majority of the people who live in this country.

Another Conservative MP, John Hall, representing Wycombe, was even more willing to bow to the 'fears' of the British people:

> We cannot overwhelm ourselves with large numbers of people who, however worthy, are alien, have alien cultures, different temperaments, totally different backgrounds and habits and different ways of life. If we allow them to come in at a rate which is faster than we can absorb them, we will create a growing fear in the minds of our own people who, rightly or wrongly, say that before the end of the century there will be large minorities of alien people in various parts of the country, and they fear that the British way of life will change. That fear exists in the minds of many people and, for this reason, entry must be regulated.

For these MPs, there was no question of responding to such 'fears' by demonstrating that they were founded on false information and stimulated by political agitation. Rather, the content of public opinion had to be the object of government legislation. This meant that the 'coloured people' of 'alien culture' had to be kept out of Britain, even when they held UK passports which gave them the right to settle in Britain. Anticipating the riposte that what the public believed was an outcome of historical events, personal experience and political agitation, Maulding resorted to arguing: 'Racial prejudice is a basic human instinct; one cannot legislate it away but can only legislate to ensure that the damage which it does becomes less and less as the years pass.'

Thus, although government ministers vehemently denied that the Bill was racist, its content and passage through parliament was defended by a succession of speakers who regarded racism as natural and inevitable, and who believed that when it was expressed by 'our own people' then it was time to protect the 'British way of life' from 'alien cultures'. In a phrase, they were arguing that 'coloured people' could never be 'British'. Just 31 MPs voted against this further institutionalisation of racism in the practice of the state.

   The Commonwealth Immigrants Bill became law in the midst
of the Labour government's preparations to strengthen the
Race Relations Act (1965). It was in this context that Enoch
Powell was able to establish himself as the spokesperson for the
'British people' with his speech on 9 February. He was able to
consolidate that position with two further speeches in 1968 (one
on 20 April in Birmingham, and the other on 16 November in
Eastbourne) which attracted massive media publicity. As a
result of the Birmingham speech he was sacked from the
Shadow Cabinet. On the 7 May, a Gallup Poll revealed that 74
per cent of those questioned agreed in general with his views
and 24 per cent said they would like him to be leader of the
Conservative Party if Edward Heath retired. His popularity
continued up to and beyond the 1970 general election, and
there is strong evidence to show that this was a significant factor
in bringing about a swing to the Conservative Party which
ensured them electoral victory. Powell's rise to public prominence was interesting in that his speeches contained little that
had not been previously said by Conservative MPs or was not
Conservative Party policy. Certainly, the policy of assisted,
voluntary 'repatriation' had been repeatedly called for by right-
wing Conservative MPs since the early 1960s and had been
adopted by the Conservative Shadow Cabinet. Other MPs had
achieved 'political success' by their expression of the 'race/
immigration' theme. What was different was the way in which
these increasingly familiar elements were combined to produce
an extremely articulate and logical expression of racism, whilst
dispensing with much of the 'extreme' rhetoric of previous proponents of such views. Powell rarely made explicit use of the
idea of 'race' and made no reference in his own words to
'coloured immigrants'. But he was able to submerge the idea of
'race' in a notion of Britishness, of nation. This was done by cit-
ing the views of the 'ordinary British citizen' expressed in conversation or letter in combination with his own reference to
'alien cultures'. The crude and inconsistent racism expressed in
the factories, shopping centres and pubs was thus endorsed by
a politician who had the authority of education, political office
and a position in the Shadow Cabinet. The direct appeal to,
and legitimation of, a part of working-class experience took the
following form in the Walsall speech:

> Only this week a colleague of mine in the House of Commons
> was dumbfounded when I told him of a constituent whose
> little daughter was now the only white child in her class at
> school. He looked at me as if I were a Member of Parliament
> for Central Africa, who had suddenly dropped from the sky
> into Westminster. So far as most people in the British Isles
> are concerned, you and I might as well be living in Central
> Africa for all they know about our circumstances.

Underneath the studied logic and academic phrasing, the object
of Powell's concern – and his vision – was the same as that of
Cyril Osborne. In his speech on 20 April 1968, Powell referred
to a conversation with a constituent whom he reported as saying:

> I have three children, all of them been through grammar
> school and two of them married now, with family. I shan't be
> satisfied till I have seen them all settled overseas. In this
> country in fifteen or twenty years time the black man will
> have the whip-hand over the white man.

Later, in the same speech, this assertion was translated into his
own, apparently more neutral, terms:

> Now we are seeing the growth of positive forces acting against
> integration, of vested interests in the preservation and
> sharpening of racial and religious differences, with a view to
> the exercise of actual domination, first over fellow-
> immigrants and then over the rest of the population.

And, if this did not make the object and the message clear, it
was underlined by reference to the United States.

The success of Powell's attempt to submerge the idea of 'race'
in the idea of nation was evident in this statement by one of the
leaders of the dock workers who went on strike and marched to
Westminster in support of Powell on 23 April: 'Mr Powell
spoke his mind. He spoke for us all. He made me feel proud to
be British.'

Equally significant was that Powell's prominence was
achieved in the context of the political agitation over the arrival
of the Kenyan Asians and was increased after the Labour
government had enacted its racist legislation. By doing the latter, the Labour government reconfirmed that the number of
'coloured immigrants' in Britain was indeed 'of the essence'. It

then had little defence when Powell pointed out that the
numbers of 'coloured immigrants' continued to increase not
only because of the continuing entry of dependants, but also
because of the children born to these migrants in Britain. The
only logical solution was 'repatriation'. But to advance it, it was
necessary to contest the fact that children born of migrant
parents in Britain were British, despite the fact that they were
British citizens. The Labour government had made exactly this
case with regard to the Kenyan Asians by arguing that their
parents or grandparents had not been born in Britain. Powell
extended the racist demands by building on this argument and
claiming that these children did not become British by virtue of
being born in Britain.

Labour's new Race Relations Bill provided Powell with a
further reason for continuing his 'race/immigration' theme. He
was firmly opposed to legislation which made racial discrimination illegal. Referring to the British population, and reinforc-
ing his claim that it had become the 'persecuted minority', he
said on 20 April:

> On top of this, they now learn that a one-way privilege is to
> be established by act of parliament: a law, which cannot, and
> is not intended, to operate to protect them or redress their
> grievances, is to be enacted to give the stranger, the
> disgruntled and the *agent provocateur* the power to pillory
> them for their private actions.

With Powell and the 'race/immigration' theme so dominant, the
Labour government's attempt to redefine the political problem
in order to justify its new legislation was bound to fail. When
the government claimed that racial discrimination was widespread and a major political problem, there was plenty of
research evidence to prove it. But this evidence was inconsistent with the predominant ideological definition, a definition
which allowed Powell and other right-wing MPs to reinterpret
racial discrimination as being the legitimate behaviour of the
private individual, the right of all 'decent British citizens'.
According to Ronald Bell, Conservative MP for Beaconsfield,
in a letter to the *Times* on 11 April 1968;

> The Bill deeply encroaches upon the proper sphere of the
> freedom of the individual and, by exacerbating ill-feeling

between people of different races in this country, will lead to permanent hostility and endemic violence.

This is an excellent example of the way in which the very real problems of racism and racial discrimination were subverted into the now common-sense linkage between the idea of 'race' and violence. The government's Bill became law, but it had lost the ideological battle: political attention remained firmly focused on the question of 'numbers' and 'alien culture'.

In 1969 there was a further concession to racist pressure in the course of the debate on an Immigration Appeals Bill. The Bill aimed to introduce an appeal system for any person refused entry into Britain. The government announced a new clause which required all Commonwealth citizens who retained the right to enter Britain to obtain an 'entry certificate' before they set out. This applied primarily to dependants of migrants already in Britain and was justifed on rational/bureaucratic grounds as a means of verifying that the person had the right to enter the country. Given the continuing agitation about 'numbers' and 'evasion', this was, in practice if not in intent, a means of slowing down the arrival of the wives and children who had the right to be in Britain. An entry certificate could only be issued following an interview at a British High Commission (often hundreds of miles away from the homes of intending migrants); there were insufficient staff to deal with applications and applicants often had to wait a year or more for an interview; and the applicant had to produce written documentation to prove the connection claimed (often impossible to present because marriage or birth certificates were not issued). Although the 'entry certificate' provision did not remove a dependant's right to come to Britain, it did seriously restrict the ability to exercise that right.

State racism rationalised

The Immigration Appeals Act (1969) marked the limit of the Labour government's willingness to institutionalise racism in the practice of the state. But its willingness to move this far was more than matched by the willingness of right-wing politicians to increase their demands. Their continuing success was measured in the extent to which the policy of the Conservative Party moved further to the right. After sacking Enoch Powell from the Shadow Cabinet, Edward Heath made a speech in York, on 20 September 1968, which was devoted entirely to 'immigration'. He called for a reduction in the numbers entering Britain, both under the voucher scheme and as dependants. Moreover, without using the term 'repatriation', he stressed that it was the policy of the Conservative Party to assist migrants to return to their country of origin if they wished. With the leader of the Conservative Party now firmly in the limelight as a result of having endorsed the 'race/immigration' theme, Powell found it even easier to press his case and gain media attention. At the party's annual conference in October, he repeated warnings about Britain's future, while in November he called for the setting up of a Ministry of Repatriation. Its task would be to organise a large-scale programme of voluntary 'repatriation'. Heath responded in January 1969 by demanding that the Labour government stop all 'immigration'.

It seemed as if each speech by Powell prompted Heath to endorse an even more reactionary, racist policy. One is reminded of the ventriloquist and the dummy. As if to confirm this image, Powell made a speech in June 1969 immediately after the Immigration Appeals Bill became law, in which he cited estimates of the cost of a 'repatriation' scheme. Hence, when the Conservative Party won the 1970 general election, there was good reason to believe that the dummy might just be willing to find the £300 million that Powell believed was needed. Certainly, the 'fears' of the British people were as strong as ever. In June 1969, a Gallup Poll revealed that 54 per cent of those questioned supported Powell's idea for a grant scheme to assist 'repatriation'. This was yet another example of the way in which the media and the opinion polls were able to sanction and encourage the expression of racist opinion by, first, making Powell's views 'news' and, then, assisting their transition into public opinion by selecting them for public comment. Having been endorsed by the public, they became 'news' again because of the degree of support they had attracted. In 1970, a post-election survey revealed that 86.6 per cent of the sample believed that 'too many immigrants have been let into this country'. This demonstrated the extent of the triumph of ideology over reality.

One of the early tasks of the Conservative government was to respond to these 'legitimate fears' of the country 'bursting at the seams' with 'coloured colonial immigrants'. The Immigration Act (1971) was designed to do this by replacing all the legislation of the 1960s, and the Aliens Restrictions Act (1914), and basing immigration control around a single distinction between 'patrials' and 'non-patrials'. This meant that the distinction between aliens and Commonwealth citizens no longer applied in relation to the law concerning entry to and settlement in Britain. The language of 'patriality' was not familiar, but the idea behind it was. The term 'patrial' currently refers to a number of different categories of people, but its prime reference is to persons born, adopted, naturalised or registered in the UK, or who were born of parents one of whom had UK citizenship, or one of whose grandparents had UK citizenship. Such people have the right to live in Britain, while non-patrials (with some limited exceptions) have to obtain permission to enter and settle in Britain. The most significant exceptions are the close dependants of Commonwealth migrants who entered Britain in the 1950s and 1960s, and citizens of other EEC countries (including the Irish Republic). The only means of entry into Britain for 'non-patrials' (unless they are businessmen, students or visitors) is to obtain a work permit issued by the Department of Employment for a specific job with a specific employer for a specific period of time. The Act therefore brought all 'non-patrials' within the framework of a law identical in effect to the situation in much of the rest of Western Europe, a law which allowed employers to recruit migrant labour when they experienced a shortage of labour. In addition, the Act gave to the Home Secretary and immigration officers a wide range of discretionary powers, including, respectively, the right to deport people and to refuse entry to people. It also extended the government's powers to assist 'repatriation'.

The Act was a comprehensive rationalisation and extension of the racist legislation of the 1960s. Moreover, it was certainly a response to people's 'fears', not about immigration *per se*, but about 'coloured colonial immigrants'. The Act increased the number of people who had the right to enter and settle in Britain – but these were people who could be considered to be 'of good stock'. This was achieved by defining the idea of 'patrial' in such a way as to include the past and future children over two generations of people who migrated and migrate from Britain to Australasia, Canada, India and parts of Africa. The Home Secretary conceded in the House of Commons, on 8 March 1971, that millions of people were included in this definition and therefore had the right to enter and settle in Britain. This very substantial increase in the size of the potential number of migrants to Britain was not greeted with dismay and shock by proponents of immigration control, presumably because they were of the same 'blood and bone', as Bernard Braine had put it in 1967. This was further confirmation, if confirmation were needed, that the argument for immigration control had never been anything other than a thin veneer obscuring the specific demand that 'coloured people' be kept out of Britain. It follows that the 1971 Act cannot be viewed as legislation which was dictated solely by economic considerations. It is, of course, true that it did regulate immigration by reference to the demand of capital for labour, but this applied only to 'non-patrials'. The Act also increased the total number of people with the right to enter Britain quite independently of economic considerations. For this reason it must be viewed as embodying a contradiction between the economic and the ideological.

The Labour Party decided to vote against the Immigration Bill in the House of Commons. In the second reading on 8 March 1971, James Callaghan claimed that it was a concession to prejudice, that it did not address the new central question of citizenship, and that it would unnecessarily increase the powers of the police, employers and Home Secretary. These themes were repeated by other Labour MPs, who concluded that the Bill would make 'race relations' worse. Peter Shore and Renée Short emphasised the extent of agreement with the Conservative government when they repeated Callaghan's proud boast that immigration had always been lower under Labour governments than under Conservative governments. Thus, when Arthur Bottomley, MP for Middlesborough east, described the 'patrial/non-patrial' distinction as racist, Conservative MPs were able to charge the Labour Party with hypocrisy because of its actions in 1965, 1968 and 1969. It was this record of racist legislation that ensured that Labour's left wing were silent during the debates on the Bill. The initiative lay almost entirely with the right wing of the Conservative Party. One of the few concessions obtained by the Labour Party in the committee stage was the limitation of the definition of 'patrial' to a person born in the UK or to a Commonwealth citizen with a parent born in the UK. This turned out to be a hollow victory, as we shall see in chapter 4.

Conservative Home Secretary Maudling attempted to deny that the Bill was racist; other Conservative MPs were less embarrassed. John Hunt, MP for Bromley, argued in the House of Commons, on 8 March, that when the term 'non-patrial' was used:

> what we mean is those born with black or brown faces. It will
> enhance the honesty and credibility of our debate if that fact
> is freely and frankly acknowledged from the start. It is possible
> in some circumstances to justify control of immigration on a
> racial basis . . . This is not the first immigration Bill to be
> based on a deliberate policy of racial discrimination.

For him, the problem, and the task of the Bill, were obvious: 'I believe that it will succeed in its aim of controlling and containing the problem of coloured immigrants.' Kenneth Clarke, MP for Rushcliffe, was equally explicit. He said of the concept of 'patrial':

> In part, it recognises the somewhat different racial content of
> those people who are likely to want to come to this country
> under the grandfather Clause. It is intellectually dishonest for
> liberal opinion – as it is for illiberal opinion – to pretend that
> the debate about immigration control in this country at the
> moment centres on anything other than the racial problems
> which the country faces . . . With the unfortunate racial
> tensions which have arisen here, and which we all regret, it is
> desirable to restrict the number of coloured immigrants into
> this country, in the interests of both the black and the white
> population here, until something can be done to alleviate
> those racial tensions and alleviate the social problems in the
> cities in which immigrants are most concentrated.

Moreover, he justified his support for the Bill on the grounds that any measure to control the 'inflow of coloured immigration' should not affect those people who wanted to return to their 'homeland': 'I should regard that as a most undesirable hardship which ought not to be caused by this country in an effort to achieve a bogus uniformity in the way it treats would-be-immigrants.' Clarke was here defending the fact that the Bill increased the number of people with the right to enter and settle in Britain. The people concerned were acceptable to him because they were of the correct 'racial content'. No one rose to challenge him, and no member of the government denied that this was so.

But it was Enoch Powell who dominated the proceedings. Almost all the Labour speakers accused the government of making concessions to 'Powellism' by introducing the Bill. They were joined in this by W.F.Deedes, Conservative MP for Ashford. Powell was unconcerned. Replying on 8 March to the Home Secretary's claim that the Conservative Party, although wishing to extend the powers of the state to assist 'repatriation', had no intention of initiating 'a large-scale programme of repatriation', he said:

> Nobody who listened to what the Conservative Party has said
> on this subject, both during the general election and in the
> years before, could have supposed that there was any
> intention to limit the availability of assistance for any
> immigrant who voluntarily applied for it. Such a limitation
> would therefore in effect be a serious breach of what was
> understood to be the undertaking of this party when it went to
> the electorate.

In the third reading, on 17 June, Powell re-emphasised that the scope of the 'repatriation' provisions in the Bill were wide and that their extensive use would reduce the 'apprehensions' of the indigenous population.

The considerable degree of agreement between Powell and the Conservative government derived from the 'justifiable fears' of 'our people'. John Hunt said in the 8 March debate that the Bill was important primarily because of 'the reassurance which the measures will bring to those, particularly in our large cities, who feel themselves in danger of being swamped and overwhelmed.' There was no disagreement with the government on this point. In his winding-up speech at the end of the third reading, Reginald Maudling, in a classic illustration of the ideology which identified the 'immigrants' as the cause of all the problems, said:

> Difficulty in race relations arises from the speed of the arrival of immigrants and their concentration in certain areas. This has led to social changes being imposed on the people already living in those areas, who perhaps find it hard to accept them. One big element in this problem, as the Minister of State said, is the fear of the unknown on the part of those already here towards those coming here about what they will find when they get here.

This reference to the need to respond to 'legitimate fears' was not only a legitimation of the 'fears' that some politicians had played a major role in encouraging, but was also a repetition in a weaker form of Powell's claim that the indigenous population was now the 'persecuted minority'. It was for this reason that Maudling claimed, on 8 March, that the main purpose of the Bill was to 'give assurance to the people who were already here before the large wave of immigration that this will be the end and that there will be no further large-scale immigration.'

This was a reassurance that would subsequently place the Conservative government in a major dilemma.

Trade unions and state racism

During the 1960s, the trade union movement complied with and endorsed this institutionalisation of racism in the practice of the state. Much of its policy and practice followed the retreat from principle of the Labour Party, and the only major divergence between the two occurred over the attempt of the Labour government to strengthen the Race Relations Act (1965). There were some unions and many individual union members who opposed the support given to state racism and the complete acceptance of the 'race/immigration' frame of reference, but they remained a minority. Here, we shall be concerned with the policy of the Trade Union Congress, for although the TUC is not synonymous with the trade union movement, it does function as a leadership and a focus for the determination of general trade union policy.

The TUC opposed the Conservative Party's Commonwealth Immigrants Act on grounds similar to those expressed by the

Labour Party, including the argument that it was racist. But, when the Labour Party gained political power, the TUC quickly followed the former's retreat from principle. In 1965, the General Council of the TUC declared itself in favour of immigration control and made no reference to the fact that the legislation it was supporting was a tougher version of that which it had earlier opposed. The justification for this change of policy was that there had been an increase in the number of immigrants who lacked knowledge of the English language and of British customs. This had permitted 'an extension of their previous environments', the consequence of which was that their 'integration' was being hindered. The General Council was also concerned that the voucher scheme did not apply to dependants whose entry therefore remained uncontrolled. Clearly, for the TUC, the problem was no longer the racism practised by the state; it was now 'numbers' and the immigrants' refusal to conform to the 'British way of life'. This 'integration' theme remained dominant for a decade, but the TUC was unable to avoid the issue of racism and racial discrimination.

First, the Labour government announced in 1966 that it intended to make racial discrimination in employment and housing illegal. There followed a series of discussions between government ministers and General Council representatives in which the latter expressed their strong opposition. The General Council argued that there was no comprehensive information to document the extent of discrimination in employment, that the use of the law was inappropriate in industrial relations and that the government would create a group of privileged workers which would obstruct integration. There was much common ground here with the right wing of the Conservative Party, and it is therefore no surprise that the TUC joined forces with the Confederation of British Industry (CBI) to campaign against the Race Relations Bill. The government persisted with its plans and the TUC, with obvious reluctance, finally conceded, in 1968, that there was a role for legislation.

Second, in 1966, 1967 and 1968, delegates to the annual congress called for action to deal with racial discrimination both within and outside the labour movement. Particular reference was made to a series of incidents where West Indian and Pakistani workers had been banned from attending or joining Labour and Working Men's Clubs. In 1967, the General Council had to resort to arbitrary rulings from the chair to prevent a motion being passed which would have committed it to broad action against racial discrimination. However, in 1968 a motion calling for action within the labour movement was successful. A TUC circular expressing opposition to racial discrimination followed, but the General Council persisted in arguing that the main problem was 'integration'. 'They' were not willing to adopt 'our ways'. This was but a short step away from arguing that the problem was that the migrants had an 'alien culture'.

The TUC had little to say about immigration control. It was unhappy with the Commonwealth Immigrants Act (1968), but not because of its racist content. Its concern was mainly economic. And, when the Conservative government published its Immigration Bill in 1971, the General Council reported to Congress that:

> many aspects of government policy had not been made plain
> and the General Council decided that a simple condemnation
> of the Bill would not deal with the complex issues involved
> and that discussions should be sought with the Home
> Secretary.

Insofar as the institutionalisation of racism by the state was concerned, the TUC had nothing to say.

Conclusion

By the end of 1971, both the ideological terms of the political debate and the public, common-sense concern had been shifted considerably to the right when compared with the situation in 1962. There was now an overwhelming political and common-sense consensus that 'race/immigration' was a major issue for political policy. This consensus was effectively unchallenged except by the revolutionary left, which itself was sufficient for the challenge to be defined as 'lunacy'. The production of that consensus was the immediate result of the actions and ideological justifications of the Labour government, the tension of its relationship with the right wing of the Conservative Party and the expression of racism in the working class. The crucial turning-point was Labour's decision to endorse and strengthen the

Commonwealth Immigrants Act (1962). Having entered the ideological territory of the racists, it had very few means for resisting the continuing demand for yet more stringent controls over the entry of 'coloured colonial immigrants'. The outcome was the full institutionalisation of racism in the practice of the state by 1971.

But the difference between the situation in 1962 and 1971 was not only that the Labour Party had endorsed the 'race/immigration' interpretation. There had also been significant developments in the content of that interpretation. First, by the turn of the decade, there was an emerging consensus between the two main political parties that a major political objective was the need to respond to the 'real and justifiable fears' of 'our people'. This consensus obscured a complex ideological situation. It ensured that the opinions and circumstances of 'our people', the British, were elevated to a determinant role in political policy. The content of those opinions was thereby subordinated to the argument about the primacy of the democratic process.

Insofar as the content of those opinions was made explicit, the consensus view was that the British people had come to fear that their 'way of life' was being changed, their 'culture' was being 'swamped' as a consequence of the 'tidal wave' of immigration. Underneath this prevalent language of nation and culture, another notion was in play. For the right wing of the Conservative Party (and for the political forces to the right of them), the real issue was that of 'race'. They did not consistently express this in public, partly because it was unnecessary (the idea of 'immigrant' now exclusively referred to 'coloured people'), and partly because it could have been counterproductive, given the proximity of the Nazi pogroms against European Jews.

Nevertheless, in the House of Commons, there was always at least one Conservative MP who would argue that immigration and its effects could only be discussed in relation to the supposed reality of 'race'. Moreover, after 1965, this claim rarely met with sustained opposition. Their argument was that the threat to the British nation and culture was grounded in the 'fact' that the migrants were of a different 'race'. Thus, they continued, the migrants caused a 'race relations' problem because they were of different 'stock'. In this interpretation, the notions of 'race' and culture were interdependent. The idea of 'race' could be contained and transmitted in the idea of 'alien culture' and vice versa. This world-view of the right was able to thrive in a political environment in which a major chapter of British history concerned the relations of 'race' in the colonies, and in which the regulation of relations between the 'races' at home had become a matter of legislation (the Race Relations Acts of 1965 and 1968). Thus, the roots of the racist beliefs and demands of the right went very deep and were nourished by the continuing legitimation of the idea of 'race' in so many facets of political life. And it was this group of people who had the political initiative.

A major consequence of this consensus on the need to respond to the 'legitimate fears' of the British people was that their racist content was obscured. This consensus therefore pre-empted any attempt to redirect political attention towards the real problem and underlaying ideological dynamic, racism. The fact that the opinions of the British people were the focus of political action ensured that both the leadership of the main political parties and the right wing had managed to occupy the ideological ground upon which they were most vulnerable to attack. At the beginning of the 1970s, the predominant reply to the accusation of racism was still an absolute denial. Maudling's reference to 'racial prejudice' being 'instinctive' pointed the way forward to a new formulation that was to develop in the new decade.

The second qualitative change was the extent to which the political debate had been shifted beyond immigration control, while retaining it as both cause and, in a negative way, solution. By the mid-1960s, immigration control had been effective in reducing to almost zero the number of 'coloured immigrants' entering Britain to work. However, the dependants of earlier migrants continued to arrive, and the reunited or newly formed families were producing children. Therefore, insofar as there was a consensus on numbers being 'the essence', the 'problem' remained. Powell was important in that he was largely responsible for directing political and public attention to these new features of the situation. Relentlessly, he drew out the logic of the racist case, arguing that the threat to the British 'way of life' could only be eliminated by 'repatriation'. The Conservative government, committed to responding to 'legitimate fears', was not yet prepared to take that next step. The institutionalisation of racism had been completed under cover of the philosophy of 'integration', which entailed a public commitment to ensuring that 'coloured immigrants' already in Britain were treated as British citizens. The contradictions of government policy and ideology were now clearly exposed, and led the Conservative government towards conflict with Powell and the forces further to his right should it refuse to follow through the logic of the racist case.

4. The drift towards 'repatriation': 1971–83

Introduction

The 1970s and the early 1980s witnessed the reinforcement of the ideological domination of the 'race/immigration' theme and the persistence of the demand for 'repatriation'. This has been accompanied by yet further restrictions on the entry of 'coloured colonial immigrants' and, since the late 1970s, a clear ideological shift to the right by the leadership of the Conservative Party. Additionally, migrants and their children have been increasingly described and understood as law-breakers, prone to violence and generally troublesome. The process of such a criminalisation was not, in itself, new. As we have seen, there were a series of questions in the House of Commons in the 1950s about the role of West Indians in certain types of crime. During the 1970s, however, it did become more systematic – partly as a response to the growing political resistance to racism amongst both the migrants and their children.

There was a consistency to these political and ideological developments insofar as they were all aspects of the continuing shift to the right. However, this consistency was fractured by a shift in the political position of the Labour Party and the official leadership of the trade union movement from the mid-1970s. It was prompted by a realisation that a growth of racist and fascist forces was occurring outside the arena of parliamentary politics and that this, if unchallenged, could come to pose a major threat to the labour movement. There was an equally sudden re-examination of policy and a number of new political initiatives, including a campaign against racism, but neither occurred in conjunction with or stimulated a wide-ranging critique of previous policy and practice. Rather, what had previously been supported was now opposed. Thus, by the early 1980s, the Labour Party was calling for the right of entry and settlement in Britain of East African Asians holding UK passports, a right that it had itself withdrawn in 1968. In the absence of a clear statement of motive, an admission of having bowed in the past to racism, and an explicit rejection of the 'race/immigration' interpretation, this change in policy could carry little credibility. Moreover, it allowed the Conservative Party to claim consistency for its own racist policies. This contradiction in the politics and ideology of the Labour Party, and the shift to the right by the Conservative Party were both constituent elements of a wider process which Stuart Hall has called 'The Great Moving Right Show'.

Continuing political agitation in the 1970s and early 1980s around the 'race/immigration' theme occurred in the context of very strict, and racist, immigration control. Consequently, 'immigration control' was less and less capable of satisfying the 'legitimate fears' of 'our own people' about the increasing size of the 'coloured population'. The 'fears' remained and were kept alive by the continuing activities of the right and the increasing inability of capitalism to provide adequate housing, employment or social services for a large proportion of Britain's population. The conditions therefore existed for the 'repatriation' solution to be articulated with even greater common-sense validity. Moreover, 'muggings' and 'race riots' replaced 'illegal immigration' as topics of widespread public anxiety and horror. These 'new problems' would 'obviously' be eliminated if those who engaged in them were 'sent back to their own country'. The events that we now outline are therefore a crucial part of a gradual drift towards the conditions that would culminate in a policy of 'repatriation'.

' . . . No further large-scale immigration'

The Conservative government justified the Immigration Act (1971) as an attempt to avert, once and for all, the 'legitimate fears' of 'our people' by assuring them that there would be 'no further large-scale immigration'. It was a clear and unambiguous promise, but one that was to prove hollow as a result of new developments in East Africa. In late 1970, there had been quiet discussions between the Conservative government and the government of Dr Milton Obote in Uganda over the problem of the limited take-up of Ugandan citizenship by people of

Asian descent. The Conservative government was predictably concerned about the numbers of UK actual or potential passport holders amongst the Asian population in Uganda. As a result of the discussions, there was an outline agreement that the position of the majority of the Asians would be regularised as far as citizenship was concerned, while for those who definitely wished to leave Uganda, there would be an increase in the number of special vouchers to allow entry to Britain. The government, mindful of its electoral promises, was slow in ratifying the agreement. In the interim, Dr Obote was overthrown by General Idi Amin, in January 1971. By the end of the year, Amin was making threatening noises about the Asian presence in Uganda. The political situation in Uganda remained uncertain for several months until August 1972, when Amin suddenly announced that Asians must leave Uganda within three months.

This posed a dilemma for the Conservative government. On the one hand, Asian UK passport holders no longer had the right to enter and settle in Britain (although there were now 3,000 vouchers available on an annual basis); while on the other, they were being expelled from Uganda. They were, therefore, about to become political refugees with UK passports that were worthless in principle, and of little value in practice (given the limit on the number of vouchers). But this was not how the situation was understood in Britain. The 'race/ immigration' interpretation predominated: people who were, in reality, political refugees were understood, ideologically, as yet another group of 'coloured colonial immigrants' who would 'swamp our culture'. Most political and press reaction was extremely hostile to the idea of any sort of concession by a government which had come to power and passed the Immigration Act (1971) on a promise of responding to 'our people's fears' about 'large-scale immigration'. None of this racist hostility and reference to election promises could alter the fact that a large proportion of those to be expelled from Uganda had, or were entitled to have, a UK passport.

Enoch Powell added his voice to the media and public clamour. Although the right-wing and racist lobby were extremely strong, so were the pressures arising from humanitarian considerations, the dishonour of broken commitments to UK passport holders, and international reaction. The Conservative government conceded to those pressures. Predictably, people whose fears had been legitimated by the government in 1970 and 1971 were furious, and many turned first to Powell, and then to the neo-fascist National Front for support and leadership.

Powell attempted to mobilise and lead the opposition within the Conservative Party when he moved a motion at the party's annual conference in September, calling on the government to implement its election promises. He was defeated by a combination of the political centre and left of the party. This was a major setback for Powell, but a marvellous opportunity for the National Front, in alliance with Conservatives who belonged to the Monday Club, to become the focus for racist opposition to the government's decision. The National Front had reacted very quickly to the situation and had produced a leaflet entitled 'The Fight for Survival is On', which concluded:

> While you are asleep the immigrants are pouring in by the
> thousand and breeding at an incredible rate. If you – and
> thousands like you – do not organise and take action now,
> then by the time you do decide to wake up you will find
> yourself a second class citizen in your own country,
> dispossessed of your birthright by teeming millions of
> coloured aliens.

The content of the message was little different from that which others had been expressing since the late 1950s, but the language was more extreme. Moreover, the National Front made no attempt to conceal its belief that 'coloured immigration' was a threat to the 'racial purity' of the British. In that relay race on a course which stretched away to the right, the baton was now in the hand of the neo-fascists, having previously been monopolised by exchanges between the Conservative and Labour governments.

The politics of the latter months of 1972 were dominated by the 'race/immigration' theme, aided by racist reporting and cartoons in the right-wing national newspapers and considerable coverage of the National Front. There was, however, a major political conflict between centre/liberal opinion, led and sanctioned by the Conservative government, and the right. Although the government carried the day insofar as the

Ugandan Asians were admitted to Britain, the ideological battle was won by the right. In September 1972, a Gallup Poll revealed that 57 per cent of those questioned were opposed to the government's decision and that 58 per cent believed that cash payments should be made to 'help immigrants who will return to their own country of origin'. The right wing of the Conservative Party and the National Front could legitimately claim that they spoke for the majority of 'our people' now that the government had broken faith. Having played a major role in cultivating the 'fears' of 'swamping', the Conservative government had to pay the cost, and watch the Monday Club and the National Front carry off the prize.

The cost was not only widespread hostility (motivated by, or expressive of, racism) in the country at large, but also in the House of Commons. In November, the government was faced with the task of carrying through the House the Immigration Rules that would determine the day-to-day operation of the Immigration Act. There was loud opposition from both the right wing of the Conservative Party – concerned that 'kith and kin' (the acceptable synonym for 'white race') were being denied the right of entry to Britain – and from the Labour Party – concerned that Britain would be 'flooded' with European immigrants now that negotiations were complete for Britain's entry into the European Economic Community. Together, these unholy forces brought about the defeat of the government. A major concession was to follow. On 25 January 1973, new Immigration Rules were presented to the House of Commons which allowed Commonwealth citizens with a grandparent born in the UK to enter and settle in Britain free of any restriction. This was a return to the government's original intentions when it first introduced the Immigration Bill. The new rules were accepted, and, on 26 January, the leader writer for the *Daily Express* spelt out the implications with great joy:

> Well done. The government has amply conceded the case for generous treatment of our kin in Australia, New Zealand and Canada . . . At least 8 million more people of British stock living overseas now have a freeway to the home-land. And they will enjoy a better status than Community nationals who come from Europe.

The Home Secretary gave a press conference on the day that the new rules were presented to the House of Commons. He emphasised that there would be no repeat of the government's concession to the Ugandan Asians. This, along with the new rules, was a measure of the government's concern to extend racist immigration control and so calm the 'legitimate fears' aroused by its 'capitulation'.

'Black crime shock'

The repercussions of the decision to admit the Ugandan Asians were framed entirely within the 'race/immigration' theme and so were consistent with earlier phases of the racialisation of British politics. 'Race' had again become a major topic of British political debate by means of 'immigration'. But this was not the only method by which racialisation continued in the 1970s. Political attention increasingly focused upon the 'second generation' – the children of the migrant workers from the Caribbean and the Indian sub-continent, most of whom had been born in Britain. The attention was focused on their alleged involvement in certain forms of street crime. The object of concern was almost exclusively the children of West Indian migrants and the crimes were defined as 'mugging' and 'sus'.

This renewed attempt to link 'race' with crime occurred at the same time that the 'immigration' theme had lost some of its power to define 'race' as a political problem. The only continuing 'coloured immigration' was of the dependants of earlier migrants and, although the far right wanted their entry stopped, it was nevertheless the case that the continuing 'coloured presence' in Britain was now more dependent upon the birth of children in Britain to earlier migrants. This was the focus of Powell's campaign and of the demand for 'repatriation'. 'Immigration' remains an important symbol and subject of agitation (as we shall see later in this chapter) but the 'race/crime' dualism emerges and partially predominates over the 'race/immigration' theme. We refer to this as criminalisation. This is an important ideological development because, from the early 1970s, it compounds the now successful process of racialisation, producing an even more potent ideological message, one that is hardly likely to calm the 'legitimate fears' of 'our people'.

The 'race/immigration' and the renewed 'race/crime' themes coincide in August 1972. At the same time that politicians and the media again become obsessed with an 'immigrant deluge', they also become obsessed for the first time with a 'new' crime – 'mugging'. On 15 August, an elderly man was stabbed to death late in the evening in central London and it appeared that he had been robbed. When the press reported the incident on 17 August, it was interpreted, using the words of a police officer, as a 'mugging gone wrong'. For many of the reporters, this indicated that a 'new' crime had appeared in Britain. For the following 13 months, this 'new' crime received considerable attention in Britain's newspapers and TV news programmes, coverage centring not so much on 'muggings' themselves as on the official reaction to 'muggings' – particularly the reactions of the judges, police and politicians. Thus, although statistics were produced at various stages to demonstrate the supposedly rapid increase in the number of 'muggings', the major focus was on what was called the 'war' against them, or the need to maintain 'law and order'. In short, there was a moral panic about 'mugging', in the same way that there was a moral panic about 'coloured immigrants'. These two panics merged.

What was this 'new' crime? The various incidents that were reported by the press and classified by the police as 'muggings' were usually robberies in the street which were accompanied by force or by the threat of force. This was certainly no new crime. All that was new was the use of the label itself. However, this term 'mugging' has its own history. It had come into common use in the United States in the 1940s to refer to robberies accompanied by violence on the streets of the big cities. But the incidents to which it referred had other characteristics: they occurred in the central urban areas often undergoing physical and social decline, they were usually carried out by young 'black' men, and their victims tended to be 'white'. A 'mugging' was therefore a 'race' crime that took place in the 'ghetto'. A more general meaning subsequently emerged: 'muggings' came to symbolise a more general decline in 'law and order', moral standards and even 'civilisation' itself.

Events in the United States are extensively reported and referred to in Britain, and the escalating 'drama' of the 'black ghettos' in the 1960s was no exception. Riots, 'black power' and the police wielding clubs and firing tear gas were all good media material, both visually and ideologically. This was the context for the import of the 'mugging' label into the British vocabulary in the late 1960s, but its reference remained generalised until August 1972. Its later usage required a reconstruction of reality to bring it in line with the new ideological message. Thus, the Metropolitan Police Commissioner in his annual report for 1972 reconstructed statistics for the supposed incidence of 'muggings' back to 1968; in November 1972, the Home Secretary asked police chiefs to collect 'mugging' statistics. Yet, neither before nor since has there been a legally defined crime of 'mugging'.

The fact that the crime statistics had to be 'reworked' to prove that 'muggings' were increasing dramatically as part of a wider 'crime wave' is, in itself, proof of the fact that what was of overriding importance was the message (the ideology). The content of this message is clearly revealed in the reporting of the attack and robbery of a man in Handsworth, Birmingham, on 5 November 1972. Three young boys were arrested and the case came to court in March 1973. One of the boys was sentenced to 20 years' detention, and the others to ten years' detention. Most of the newspapers concentrated first on the sentencing, having paid only peripheral attention to the original incident and court proceedings. The drama of the long sentences was subsequently displayed by a search for a wider meaning of, and explanation for, the incident itself. A number of themes were presented in this search and each newspaper organised them in a particular way. There was, however, a more general consensus that this 'mugging' was to be understood in the context of Handsworth as a 'problem area', with bad housing, few jobs and increasing crime. In short, Handsworth was a place where people were afraid to 'walk alone'. It was also an 'immigrant area'. Thus, the 'ghetto/race/crime' connection was complete. It is best illustrated by this description from the *Daily Mail* of 21 March 1973:

> All the sentenced youths are either coloured or immigrants and live in one of Birmingham's major problem areas. Police and social workers have been battling for five years to solve community problems in Handsworth, where juvenile crime steadily worsens and there are continuous complaints about

the relationship between the police and the predominantly
coloured public.

'Mugging' entered common-sense thinking in this way, accompanied by the ideas of 'race' and 'ghetto'. It was a magnificent
'confirmation' of the prediction by Powell, the Monday Club
and the National Front: the problem at the heart of American
cities would be transferred to Britain if 'immigration' was not
stopped and 'repatriation' not begun. The notion of 'waves of
immigrants' overlapped with the idea of 'crime wave', giving
added impetus to the claim that 'our decent and law-abiding'
people were being swamped. Moreover, what they were being
swamped by was made more specific: it was not only the 'teem-
ing millions', but also young 'black' men from the 'ghetto'.

Since 1972–3, 'mugging' panics have come and gone. Periodically, the police, press and politicians will conclude that 'mugging' is a major problem, and a similar set of meanings and
images will be reproduced for public consumption. More consistently, the right wing of the Conservative Party and the neo-
fascists make their case for 'repatriation' either by enquiring
about, or stating a link between, 'race' and crime. In the case
of the latter, the periodic agitation about 'black muggers' is no
more than an expression of their consistent and explicit racism.
The first moral panic about 'mugging' occurred at a time of
rapidly deteriorating relations between the police and West
Indians, particularly the children of West Indian migrants.
Official recognition of this is evident in the fact that the House
of Commons Select Committee on Race Relations and Immigration (*sic*) had chosen 'police/immigrant relations' as its topic
for investigation in 1971. The committee's report noted that a
large majority of witnesses believed that relations between the
police and young West Indians were very bad, while much of
the submitted evidence recorded a long history of police harassment. Other studies record a similar picture.

It is, therefore, highly significant that before the police publicly labelled a particular robbery with violence as a 'mugging',
in August 1972, they had already organised special squads in
London to apprehend 'muggers'. The focus of much of their
activity was south London; the people they were apprehending
were young West Indians. This was confirmed by a leading

member of one of these 'anti-mugging' squads who agreed in court that he was particularly concerned to watch for 'coloured young men'. Consequently, it is as a result of a specific police decision, at a particular point in time, that there was a moral panic about 'mugging'. Furthermore, that operational decision occurred at a time when the police were themselves the object of political attention as a result of allegations of harassment.

An almost identical pattern of events occurred in 1982. Lord Scarman's report on the 1981 Brixton riots had identified racism in the police force as a contributory factor to the cause of the riots, and had made a number of recommendations to attempt to eradicate it. The police were again on the defensive. On 21 January 1982, the *Daily Mail* carried a story, headlined 'More and More Muggings but the Yard Fights Back', which reported that a senior Metropolitan police officer was of the opinion that the operations against 'muggers' should continue, despite the Scarman Report's criticisms. Throughout February and March, the right-wing press published reports about 'mugging': 'Muggings Double Since Brixton Riots' (*Daily Telegraph*, 4 February 1982); 'Menace of the Muggers' (*Sun*, 18 February 1982); 'A Mugging Every Half-an-Hour' (*Daily Express*, 8 March 1982). A number argued that the alleged rapid increase in 'muggings' called for a reconsideration of the conclusions of the Scarman Report. The message was that the major problem was 'black crime' and not police harassment.

On 10 March, the Metropolitan police released statistics on recorded crime in London in 1981 to a selected group of journalists. The following day, the press duly reported: 'Black Crime: The Alarming Figures' (*Daily Mail*); 'The Yard Blames Black Muggers' (*Sun*); 'Yard Reveals Race Link in Street Crime Explosion' (*Daily Express*). The basis for these headlines was the decision of the Metropolitan police to highlight the statistics on 'robbery and other violent theft' and to record the 'appearance of the assailant' for this category of recorded crime. Asked why the police had chosen this particular emphasis, Deputy-Assistant Commissioner Kelland said that it was a response to 'public opinion and pressure' as reflected in the media. In other words, the police responded to the 'legitimate fears' of 'our people' as expressed in newspaper stories in the *Daily Telegraph*, *Sun*, *Daily Express* and *Daily Mail*.

The police decision to focus public attention in this manner was racist. The statistics do not permit such simplistic conclusions and, insofar as they do present a clear picture, it is rather different from that drawn by Deputy-Assistant Commissioner Kelland. First, criminal statistics are inherently misleading. They deal only with reported crime and obscure the fact that police activity itself can lead to an increase in the reporting of certain types of crime. Second, there is no crime of 'mugging'. The police image of 'mugging' is of a robbery in the street involving violence, but the statistical category 'robbery and other violent theft' includes incidents such as 'snatches' (where no violence is used), robberies from business premises and 'other robberies' which do not occur on the street. Hence, the offence understood as 'mugging' in fact referred to only 31 per cent of the total of this general statistical category. Crimes understood as 'muggings' amounted to 0.9 per cent of the total of recorded serious offences and were, therefore, only a tiny fraction of the serious offences reported in London in 1981.

Third, the explicit racialisation of one particular set of statistics was based upon the 'victim's perception' of the person committing the offence. Yet eye-witness evidence is notoriously unreliable, and the statistics refer only to those *alleged* to have been involved, and not to those charged or convicted. Moreover, when under pressure, the police subsequently released statistics referring to the physical appearance of 'mugging' victims: nearly 18 per cent were classified as 'black', Arab or Chinese. Additionally, police statistics for 1979 and 1980 showed that there were more 'black' victims of recorded assaults, robberies and other violent offences than the total number of the incidents which are popularly known as 'muggings'.

Finally, for the offences which were numerically far more important than 'robbery and other theft', the Metropolitan police released no information on the physical appearance of the alleged criminal. One can only conclude that the decision to draw attention to the physical appearance of the alleged attacker in connection with just one category of crime was politically motivated by a desire to encourage 'public opinion' to come to racist conclusions.

None of this denies that crimes labelled as 'muggings' occur.

Neither does it deny that some young people of West Indian ancestry do commit such offences. But public opinion had become concerned about 'mugging' to the exclusion of other forms of crime (which are far more common) as a result of a decision by the police and the reporting of right-wing newspapers. Moreover, the 'mugger' had been stereotyped as a young West Indian, quite contrary to the facts (including a Home Office study) via the same channels. This is what we call the conjunction of criminalisation and racialisation. The same process occurred with another offence, that of being a suspected person.

Under Section 4 of the Vagrancy Act, it was an offence to be a 'suspected person . . . with intent to commit (an arrestable offence)'. To be arrested as a 'suspected person', an individual had to be observed acting in a suspicious manner on at least two separate occasions, although these needed only to be minutes apart. Where a person was charged with this offence, the case usually proceeded in front of a magistrate, with the only evidence provided by two police officers. It was therefore an offence which gave the police wide powers. By the mid-1970s, it had become apparent that a large proportion of the people charged under Section 4 of this Act were 'black', usually boys of West Indian ancestry. For example, statistics produced in a written answer in the House of Commons in December 1978 showed that 44 per cent of all 'sus' arrests in the Metropolitan police area in 1977 were of 'black-skinned' people. However, the statistics also showed that the total numbers arrested for this crime varied from area to area, as did the numbers and proportion who were 'black-skinned'.

The evidence suggested that this was another instance in which the police in certain areas were labelling young people of West Indian ancestry as criminals. The police claimed that the arrest pattern was no more than a reflection of the disproportionate involvement of young West Indians in certain forms of street crime. However, a report prepared by the Runnymede Trust in 1976 pointed out that:

> It is not possible to tell how indiscriminate the police are being in their use of the law. There have been a number of cases of obvious abuse and it is possible that the police are

more concerned with asserting their control over blacks on
the streets than with the niceties of being certain that the
youth in question was intending to commit an offence at the
moment when he was arrested. What is certain is that the
black community believes that the law is being used in this
way.

Indeed, the same report cited the example of a youth, subsequently acquitted, being told by the magistrate that West
Indian youths who visited the West End of London were 'asking
for trouble'. Moreover, it suggested that the workings of the
magistrates' courts were not an appropriate means of determining the validity or otherwise of the 'sus' charge:

It is rarely possible to tell from the evidence before the court
whether or not the defendant was intending to commit an
offence; the interpretation of his actions is likely to depend on
whether your sympathies lie with the police or with the
defendant. For the magistrate, institutional pressures are
likely to make him more ready to believe the police, and the
burden of proof is therefore effectively on the defendant to
prove his innocence. Particularly as there are rarely any
independent witnesses.

Even if sections of the police were not using the Vagrancy Act
as a cover for racist harassment, the wide degree of individual
interpretation involved in bringing the charge, in combination
with the workings of the magistrates' courts, ensured that con-
clusive proof of the police's defence against this charge could
not be obtained. It was therefore no surprise that large sections
of the West Indian population were concluding that the British
legal system was racist. By the late 1970s, a Black People's
Organisations' Campaign Against Sus was campaigning, along
with many other organisations, for the abolition of the offence.

It was not until May 1980 that a parliamentary committee
came to similar conclusions. The Select Committee on Home
Affairs then recommended the immediate repeal of Section 4 of
the 1824 Vagrancy Act, claiming: 'it is not in the public interest
to make behaviour interpreted as revealing criminal intent, but
equally open to innocent interpretation, subject to criminal
penalties.' The police strongly objected, predicting an increase
in street crime if the recommendation was implemented. The
Conservative government agreed to repeal Section 4; it also

decided to create a new offence. Thus, the Criminal Attempts Act (1981) made it an offence for a person to interfere with a motor vehicle with the intention of gaining entry or access to something in it. The generality of the offence and the fact that it remained open to police interpretation with little or no additional evidence was sufficient for those who had campaigned about the 'sus' law to continue their action.

The 'mugging' panics, the use of the 'sus' law and a variety of other aspects of police policy and behaviour (including the use of the Special Patrol Group in London) have led to a massive breakdown in relations between the police and communities in certain areas of migrant settlement. Thus, just a month before the April 1981 riots in Brixton, a report of the Working Party into Police/Community Relations in Lambeth claimed that the relations between police and public were 'extremely grave'. What happened in April proved that they were correct. However, the political success of the 'law and order' theme in the hands of a right-wing Conservative government and the police has meant that the process of criminalisation has continued.

In March 1983, Harvey Proctor, MP for Basildon, asked a series of written questions in the House of Commons about criminal statistics for the Metropolitan area, and made special reference to 'ethnic appearance'. If there was any doubt about what was meant by this vague term, Proctor clarified the situation by asking the government minister, on 28 March, 'if he will hold a public inquiry into the increases in offences of robbery and other violent theft committed by coloured people in the Metropolitan police districts; and if he will make a statement.' The press reacted selectively to the mass of information that Proctor's questions on 9, 28 and 31 March revealed: 'Fury Over Blacks and Crime' (London *Standard*, 23 March 1983); 'Black Crime Shock' (*Sun*, 23 March 1983); 'Storm Over Black Muggings' (*Sun*, 24 March 1983).

These newspapers made no reference to the fact that these same statistics revealed, for example, that 69 per cent of arrests for violence against a police officer were of people who were 'white'. They also failed to take account of the significance of the statement by Mr Mayhew, Minister of State at the Home Office, that: 'The reliability of the victim's assessment of the ethnic appearance of an assailant will depend on the circumstances of the offence. This weakness must be borne in mind in the interpretation of any statistics based on this information.' However, Mayhew conceded the case to Proctor when he referred to the overriding importance of 'public opinion' as justification for releasing statistics: 'but these statistics give the best information which is available on a matter of current public concern.'

The format of these statistics was the same as for those which had been released in March 1982, and so was subject to exactly the same objections. In the light of hostile reaction against the statistics and the way in which they were used, the Home Office decided against publication. That they had been collected was nevertheless made known to certain Conservative MPs by certain senior police officers. Following Proctor's question, the significance and strength of 'public concern' was sufficient to force Mayhew to release them and to set the process of racialisation and criminalisation in motion again. Proctor's interest has to be considered in relation to his membership of the right-wing Monday Club and his support for 'voluntary repatriation'. Indeed, his politics are sufficiently far to the right for him to have received the support of the Young National Front paper, *Bulldog*, in the general election of 1983. (In 1982, the editor of this paper had been imprisoned for six months after conviction on eight counts of 'incitement to racial hatred'.)

There was, needless to say, little 'public concern' over the results of an enquiry into violent attacks on West Indian and Asian people. Published a little earlier, the enquiry (which the Home Office had been forced to conduct) showed that Asians were 50 times more likely, and other 'black' people 36 times more likely, to be the victims of racist attacks than 'white' people. Nevertheless, the study recorded a tendency for both the police and local authorities to regard attacks on Asians as somehow offset by 'alleged anti-social activities of young West Indians'. If the police and local authorities do operate on the basis of such assumptions, it provides further evidence of the 'institutionalisation of criminalisation' of New Commonwealth migrants and their children, particularly male, West Indian youth.

Such criminalisation was a major ideological dimension of politics in the 1970s and early 1980s. But this did not displace the 'race/immigration' theme. Rather, it remained implicit in the criminalisation process: without 'immigration' there would be no 'race relations' problem in Britain, without a 'race relations' problem there would be no 'mugging'. Moreover, it periodically emerged as the object of political debate in its own right. During Labour's 1974–9 government, this happened as a result of an attempt to pursue a more 'liberal' policy of racist control, although the structure of state racism remained completely intact.

Labour in power again: facing in opposite directions

The Labour government of the mid-1970s implemented contradictory policies with limited strain: it maintained the structure of immigration control which had been established to keep 'coloured immigrants' out of Britain, and yet campaigned against racism. Although opposed to the 1971 Immigration Act, the government did not regard its abolition as a matter of high priority. It committed itself to a review of nationality law and to a principle of defining the right of entry into Britain by reference to citizenship (and not by patriality). It made little progress in achieving these objectives beyond the publication of a discussion document. This was all symptomatic of its minority position in the House of Commons, and the fact that it staggered from one crisis to another. In turn, this reflected the fact that Labour lacked credibility as an electoral alternative to the Conservative Party.

Throughout the 1970s, close dependants of earlier New Commonwealth migrants retained the right to enter Britain, but the entry certificate system was effective in reducing the number because of the reasons outlined on page 67. Those with a legal right to enter Britain were, at best, prevented for long periods from exercising that right and, at worst, barred from entry. For example, in September 1974, applicants for an entry certificate had to wait 18 months for an interview at the British High Commission in Karachi. At other High Commissions in the Indian sub-continent in the course of the 1970s, the delay was anything up to three years. Moreover, a study was conducted in 1976 of 58 cases where an entry certificate had been refused and where an appeal against that decision had also been refused. The

researchers visited the applicants' villages, in Pakistan, and discovered that, in 55 cases, the applicant did have a genuine right
of entry into Britain.

The government appeared to commit itself to reform. Soon
after its election, it announced its intention to increase the
number of staff dealing with applications in the Indian sub-continent. In January 1975, Alex Lyon (Minister of State at the
Home Office) visited the Indian sub-continent to observe the
situation and procedures at first hand. Following his visit, a
number of changes were made to the procedure by which an
entry certificate was issued or refused. The overall result was a
limited reduction in the waiting time for interview and a small
fall in the percentage of applications refused. Lyon made a
strong public commitment to these reforms, arguing that those
with a right to live in Britain should not be subjected to
unnecessary delay in exercising it. He was sacked in April 1976,
and thereafter the proportion of applicants refused an entry certificate increased. By December 1978, there had been slight
reductions in waiting times when compared with the situation in
1974, but at Dacca, Islamabad and Karachi, it was still more
than 18 months.

These contradictory initiatives on entry certificates were
symptomatic of policy and practice under Labour. There were
other 'liberal' initiatives. For example, on 29 August 1974, new
immigration rules were published which allowed entry to husbands and fiancés of women living in Britain. This restored a
right taken away by the previous Labour government. On 6
February 1975, the Home Secretary announced that the
number of special vouchers available for UK passport holders
denied the right to enter Britain would be increased from 3,500
to 5,000 each year. In November 1977, the government
announced an extension of the amnesty to Commonwealth and
Pakistani citizens who had entered Britain illegally before 1
January 1973. Finally, the government considerably strengthened the legislation which made racial discrimination illegal
and set up the Commission for Racial Equality to replace both
the Race Relations Board and the Community Relations Commission. This was all implemented in a new Race Relations Bill
which became law in 1976.

These 'reforms' occurred within the framework of a continu-

ing public commitment to a policy of 'strict immigration control', a now well-understood synonym for a policy of keeping
out 'coloured immigrants'. On 22 March 1977, the government
produced amended Immigration Rules to respond to another
moral panic about immigration control, this time concerning
alleged marriages of convenience. Under the new rules, a husband married to a women settled in Britain, but whose marriage
had taken place less than 12 months before entry into Britain,
could only be admitted for 12 months in the first instance; a
fiancé could be admitted for only three months initially. Then,
in January 1979, came the revelation that a number of women
from the Indian sub-continent had been forced to undergo
gynaecological examination at Heathrow and in India and Pakistan. The justification for this examination was that it would
establish whether or not the woman was a virgin, the implication being that a woman who was not and who was entering
as a fiancée of a man settled in Britain was necessarily an illegal
entrant. Although the Home Secretary announced, on 2 February, that gynaecological examinations were to be stopped, he
also later made it clear that the Immigration Rules had permitted such examinations. In the course of the political row over
this revelation, it also became known that X-ray examinations
were being conducted in Bangladesh in an attempt to establish
the age of intending entrants. This practice continued despite
the fact that experts believed such examinations to be accurate
to within only four years; they also exposed people, especially
pregnant women, to unnecessary health dangers. On 19 February, an enquiry into the use of X-ray examinations was
announced.

Thus, the 'reforms' of the early period of the Labour government were counteracted by policy in the later period. The former were stimulated by pressure from the left of the Labour
Party and by a growing realisation that 'coloured immigrants'
had votes which needed to be won. Yet there was no full-scale
assault on the ideological justification for its policy. Moreover,
there were other pressures which tended in the other direction.
Even the 'reforms' ensured that the 'race/immigration' theme
remained an object of political debate, and that 'public opinion'
continued to be exercised about it. Additionally, the right wing
of the Conservative Party and Enoch Powell (who had now left

the Conservative Party) continued their agitation and speeches on behalf of that 'public opinion'. Powell's speeches repeated his, by now, well-known themes. On 27 February 1975, he spoke at a meeting of Monday Club branches in Croydon, and claimed:

> the 'best people' of all parties and of none have succeeded in burying out of sight the greatest problem overhanging the future of Britain, a problem infinitely more grave and intractable then energy or inflation or balance of payments or any of the other ephemera that fill the media and reverberate month after month in public debate.

The 'prospective magnitude of the New Commonwealth element in England' remained his concern and he called for 'a planned movement of population' to deal with this 'grave problem'. In February 1976, he spoke at Egham Rotary Club, calling for the withdrawal of the right of entry of close dependants. He returned to the topic of 'repatriation' in a speech to the Surrey branch of the Monday Club in Croydon, on 4 October, where he suggested a scheme whereby Asian and West Indian migrants and their children born in Britain (the 'alien wedges') be given £1,000 per person to return to their 'country of origin'. Only with such a scheme, Powell continued, would it be possible to avoid violence. On 22 January 1977, this prediction was repeated in a speech to Stretford Young Conservatives: 'violence on a disastrous scale is virtually certain if the "alien wedges" . . . in the metropolis and other major English cities and towns increase at the predictable rate.'

Powell still had allies in the Conservative Party in the House of Commons, much of whose activity consisted of asking a string of questions around the 'race/immigration' theme. For example, on 28 October 1975, John Stokes, MP for Halesowen and Stourbridge, asked for statistics on the number of New Commonwealth immigrants who had been accepted for settlement in 1975. On the same day, John Biggs-Davison, MP for Epping Forest, asked for a statement on the numbers of immigrants assisted with 'repatriation' in 1974 and 1975 and, as a supplementary question: 'how many wives and children of immigrants settled on 1 January 1973 may still claim admission to the United Kingdom; and whether they are fully listed?' On

12 February 1976 Phillip Goodhart, MP for Bromley, asked when the admission of dependants and UK passport holders in East Africa would be complete, and, 'As polygamy is legal in a number of Commonwealth countries, will the Minister give an assurance that second wives and the children of second marriages are not included in the list of those eligible for entry?' This question was especially successful in linking the idea of the 'never-ending stream' with the notion of 'alien culture'. Nick Budgen, MP for south-west Woverhampton, asked, on the same occasion, about new instructions to immigration officers and enquired whether 'the spirit of these fresh instructions is "If in doubt, let them in".' Sir Bernard Braine, MP for south-east Essex, added his voice to the clamour for information by asking what success the goverment had had in dealing with illegal immigration in 1975 and 1976.

Persistent questioning of the government is an important means of trying to ensure that a given issue remains the object of political debate. By asking these particular questions, the right wing of the Conservative Party was able to maintain pressure on the Labour government on the 'race/immigration' theme. This pressure was not, however, in the public view: parliamentary written questions and answers are reported in the media only in the most exceptional circumstances. Unexpected events and deliberate action by some right-wing Conservative MPs and Enoch Powell made 'race/immigration' the object of widespread media and public attention for much of 1976. These developments put the Labour government firmly on the defensive.

On 17 May 1976, the British press reported that some 250 UK passport holders of Asian origin were being expelled from Malawi for political reasons. Soon, the 'legitimate fears' about another 'tidal wave' had been revitalised – despite the fact that those expelled were able to enter Britain as part of the overall annual quota of 5,000 vouchers available to UK passport holders of Asian origin. This gave added impetus to those right-wing Conservative MPs who had arranged a debate in the House of Commons on 24 May to discuss the 'changing demographic character of Britain'. On that day, Jonathan Aitken, MP for east Thanet, moved this motion:

> That this House notes with concern the changing
> demographic character of Great Britain, particularly the
> outflow of young people emigrating overseas and the
> continuing inflow of immigrants from the New
> Commonwealth; and calls on the Government, in the
> interests of improving race relations, to make a clear and
> accurate statement of its immigration policy.

He claimed that there was a danger of a 'sleepwalk' into a 'change of our national character' and a growing public awareness of a relaxation of immigration control which 'has had an adverse psychological impact on the indigenous population which has been detrimental to good race relations.' He added that 'race relations' had been transformed into 'a dry and brittle scrubland of tension which could be set ablaze at any moment by a spark of fear, anger and misunderstanding.' He then provided his own sparks of misunderstanding. He argued that entry to Britain should not be 'a passport to free loading on the Welfare State', that verbal evidence from the Metropolitan police suggested a 'massive immigrant smuggling racket' leading to 'thousands' of illegal migrants entering Britain annually and that the numbers of dependants and overstayers were proving problematic.

The motion was supported by Robert Mellish, Labour MP for Bermondsey, who expressed outrage at the entry of the Malawi Asians: 'Problems at local level will become worse and worse for our own people unless something is done . . . People cannot come here just because they have a British passport – full stop.' Powell followed with a reference to a confidential report from the Foreign Office in support of his claim that there was a 'limitless and continuing influx'. On this occasion, he was explicit in identifying the cause of the problem when he alluded to 'the continual increase towards the estimate of a former Home Secretary that one-third of major towns and cities and industrial areas in our country will be coloured.'

It was now clear that, for Aitken, Mellish and Powell, the 'changing demographic character' meant a decline in the proportion of 'our people' and an increasing proportion of 'coloured people'. Powell took the argument a stage further than the previous speakers. The 'inexorable build-up' of the 'coloured population', he continued, was leading to a major transformation of English cities

> where assaults upon the police are matters of daily occurrence and where in daylight, let alone after dark, ordinary citizens are unwilling and afraid to go abroad . . . With communities which are so divided nothing can prevent the injection of explosives and fire-arms with the escalating and self-augmenting consequences which we know perfectly well from experience in other parts of the United Kingdom and the world.

Thus, from behind an array of statistics on percentage births to New Commonwealth mothers, there emerged an additional allegation for which no supporting evidence was offered. For Powell, the 'limitless' increase in the 'coloured population' in English cities was accompanied by a breakdown in 'law and order'. He was continuing within the House of Commons the process of criminalisation which had been initiated by the police and the media.

The rest of the debate was comparatively inconsequential. Labour MPs attempted to show that the allegations about the numbers of immigrants were unfounded and to defend their conception of a 'multi-racial and multi-cultural society'. They argued that the level of immigration was determined by two 'inescapable commitments'. Ronald Bell, Conservative MP for Beaconsfield, dissented, claiming that there was no commitment or legal requirement to allow the entry of UK passport holders of Asian origin, also implying that the British-born children of New Commonwealth migrants were 'immigrants'. William Whitelaw, summing up for the Conservative Opposition, did not openly dissent. His main concern was to calm the 'fears' of 'our people' by guaranteeing strict control of immigration. He called for a reduction in the annual quota of vouchers for UK passport holders, and expressed concern about the continuing flow of dependants, overstaying and illegal entrants. Home Secretary Roy Jenkins approved it all by saying that it was the government's policy to maintain 'strict immigration control' and 'root out' illegal immigrants and overstayers. He concluded: 'I have not sought to disguise the fact that immigration is one of the most intractable problems which successive Governments have had to face.' This, and the fact that the motion was approved without a division, was a major endorsement of the 'race/immigration' theme and a significant concession to the right wing of the Conservative Party.

Within a fortnight of this debate and the wide media coverage given to Powell's speech, Gurdip Singh Chaggar was stabbed to death in broad daylight in Southall, London. Two days later, on 6 June, over 200 Asians staged a demonstration outside Southall police station. On 13 June, around 7,000 people marched through Southall to protest against the murder. But the racist violence continued. On 12 June, three Asian youths were attacked on an Underground train in east London. The political initiative was quickly being taken up by forces outside parliament. In the *Sunday Times* for 6 June, a leading member of the neo-fascist National Front was reported as saying:

> I feel there is violence in the air. But don't blame us . . .
> Where we are strong, we are putting a lot of psychological
> pressure on immigrants. We are telling them we do not feel
> that they should be here. At least, our tactics are more honest
> than other politicians' . . . Yes, we are a racialist party and
> we are 'respectabilising' racism.

Indeed, that was so. But all the initial work in 'respectabilising' racism had been done in and outside the House of Commons in the preceding 20 years by Labour and Conservative politicians. The racialisation of migrant labour from the New Commonwealth had now reached a stage where ideology was being translated into political practice of a more extreme form. Verbal abuse was being replaced by physical violence. It was further proof that the argument that 'strict immigration control' was essential to maintain 'good race relations' was nonsense. The racists would not give up their agitation until 'strict immigration control' had been transformed into 'repatriation', while the continuing expression and practice of racism (including that by the state) was leading to a growing movement of resistance on the part of the migrants and their British-born children. Yet the expression of this contradiction in the events of June 1976 could be used most effectively by the right as further evidence to support their claim that conflict was the inevitable outcome of the presence of 'alien cultures' in Britain. The serious fighting that broke out on 30 August between young West Indians and the police at the end of the Notting Hill Carnival provided further material to support this view.

The right-wing Labour government, now acutely aware of its minority position in the House of Commons and firmly embracing the 'race/immigration' theme, had little room for manoeuvre. It had firmly closed the door on even a cautious shift away from the 'race/immigration' theme by sacking Alex Lyon. Yet, there was little that could be done to reduce 'coloured immigration' even further without once again breaking with previous commitments and preventing the entry of wives and children of migrants already in Britain. The government's position was clearly illustrated in the House of Commons, on 8 June, when Prime Minister James Callaghan was confronted by Sidney Bidwell, Labour MP for Southall, over the events in his constituency the previous weekend. Callaghan, naturally, deplored those events, and then commented:

> race relations in this country have been good over the years,
> thanks to the good sense and moderation of the vast majority
> of our people of all communities . . . I urge everyone not to
> allow passion to destroy our reputation as a tolerant, cohesive
> and unified society.

He concluded with a reference to the government's opposition to racial discrimination, as enshrined in the new Race Relations Bill. This was ideology of the purest kind. The 'moderation' of 'our [indigenous] people' was contradicted by the evidence of the opinion polls which showed that a majority believed that there were 'too many immigrants' in Britain and favoured a policy of 'voluntary repatriation'. And Britain's reputation as a 'tolerant society' was well tarnished when the Labour Party's Commonwealth Immigrants Act (1968) was referred to the European Commission on Human Rights on the grounds that it was racist. There was no direct condemnation of racism. There was not even a token attack on the right wing of the Conservative Party or on Powell, let alone the National Front. At this particular point in time, the ideological capitulation of the Labour government to the racist right was almost total.

The paralysis of the government was not reproduced throughout the labour movement. Ever since the 1950s, there had been a small current of left-wing opinion which had rejected the 'race/immigration' interpretation and had argued that the problem requiring political attention and action was racism. By the early 1970s, the left had had some success at local level, especially in parts of the Midlands, in committing the trade union movement to a more active, anti-racist politics. Within the TUC, the left had become sufficiently strong by 1973 to move a motion which called upon the next Labour government to repeal the Immigration Act (1971). The trade union leaders did not feel secure enough to oppose the left, not least because they had begun to fear the consequences of continuing racism and discrimination in places of work and in the trade unions. A series of industrial disputes – notably at Mansfield Hosiery Ltd, in 1972, and Imperial Typewriters Ltd, in 1973 – had publicly exposed trade union complicity in racist practices and had raised the possibility of the formation of 'black' trade unions. Moreover, the dispute at Imperial Typewriters had been influenced by the neo-fascist National Front, and events since then suggested that the latter was a growing political force (see chapter 5). The leadership, at first cautious about the initiative of the left, began to move towards a more explicitly anti-racist politics. The events of June 1976 were an additional spur.

On 8 June, the Labour Party (in contrast to the Labour government) committed itself to campaign against racism and fascist violence. This followed an internal report on the growing electoral success of the National Front in local elections. Throughout the summer, local trades councils and a number of national union leaderships committed themselves to action against racism and fascism in Britain. The initiative was sustained at the 1976 annual TUC conference where an impressive array of trade union leaders followed each other to the rostrum to denounce racism, to call for the National Front to be banned and to warn their members of the divisive effects of racism within the labour movement. A series of organisational changes within the TUC was endorsed, including the setting up of a Race Relations Advisory Committee. On 3 September, a joint Labour Party/TUC campaign against racism was launched. Labour-controlled local authorities were advised not to allow racist organisations to use council buildings to hold meetings and Labour MPs and ministers were asked to speak at anti-racist meetings. The campaign culminated in the autumn with a demonstration in London attended by over 30,000 people.

Throughout 1977 and 1978, individual unions (including the National Union of Public Employees, the General and Municipal Workers' Union and the National Union of Railwaymen) urged their members to become actively involved in the struggle against racism and took action to prevent members of fascist organisations taking up official union positions. The Labour Party went on to involve itself in more broad-based initiatives. In December 1977, a meeting at the House of Commons led to the formation of a Joint Committee Against Racialism which launched a national campaign on 17 April 1978. It was supported by all three main political parties and a variety of religious and minority organisations.

This campaign and the Labour Party's involvement were prompted in part by growing support for the activities of the Anti-Nazi League, formed largely as the result of an initiative of the Socialist Workers' Party. The ANL (and its various off-shoots – including Rock Against Racism) was able to mobilise large numbers of people against the National Front, and was prepared to take direct action to prevent the NF from holding marches. Moreover, it was quick to respond to events. For example, following widespread racist violence in the East End of London on 11 June 1978, the ANL organised a protest rally for 18 June in conjunction with local Bengali organisations. Though other sections of the labour movement were slower to react, the TUC did intervene by distributing an anti-racist and anti-fascist leaflet in the area in August and September; later Bethnal Green and Stepney Trades Council published a report on racist violence in the East End.

These, and a large number of other local and national activities, constituted a significant ideological and political departure. Widely reported in the media, they represented an attempt to define racism as a major political problem – something which had not happened on a major scale in British politics. However, beyond showing that there was a substantial body of anti-racist opinion in a variety of liberal and socialist shades, their longer-term effect was not very great. This is partly because the Labour Party and TUC were initially motivated by fear of the apparently growing influence of the National Front; concern about racism was secondary, although it did become a prominent focus of the campaign. Moreover, the campaign was reactive and defensive – it was therefore difficult to encompass institutionalised state racism, and the Labour Party was unhappy about any such development. Consequently, in the rush to present the neo-fascist organisations as the main enemy, the culpability of successive Labour and Conservative governments was largely ignored. The 'race/immigration' analysis was merely displaced and was therefore unchallenged. Furthermore, during these anti-racist campaigns, the Labour government was busy strengthening racist immigration controls, as we have seen. Finally, the rightward shift within the leadership of the Conservative Party guaranteed the survival of the 'race/immigration' interpretation and its subsequent emergence in the run-up to the 1979 general election. With the election of a Conservative government in April 1979, the anti-racist and anti-fascist campaign of the labour movement came to a sudden halt. Racism and racist violence did not.

' . . . People are really rather afraid'

The sharp move to the right within the Conservative Party began in the late 1970s. On a wide range of issues, the party, now led by Margaret Thatcher, adopted radical, right-wing positions – including a determination to keep the 'race/immigration' theme at the centre of political debate. Although the Conservative Party has not yet endorsed the Powellite solution, it has moved much closer to it, and the logic of its ideology continues to point in that direction. The government argues that the 'fears of our people' about the size of the 'coloured population' and about being 'swamped' by 'alien cultures' are justified. It does so in circumstances where it is not immigration but natural reproduction which maintains that population, and therefore the 'problem' can only be resolved by a policy of 'repatriation'. This legitimation of racism is accentuated by the continuing emphasis upon immigration as a political problem, at a time when migration from the New Commonwealth consists almost entirely of dependants of men who entered Britain as migrant workers a decade previously, and at a time when over 40 per cent of the people identified in this way have been born in Britain. The language of the right wing of the Conservative Party is now widely used by its leadership, and the only significant difference between these two sections is over the policy of 'repatriation'.

The first indication of this shift to the right came in March 1977 when Margaret Thatcher was asked in the House of Commons to comment on the call for a complete ban on all further immigration from a Conservative candidate in a by-election. Her reply was that people's 'fears' could be ended only 'by holding out a clear prospect of an end to immigration'. At the party's annual conference in October, William Whitelaw predicted that a future Conservative government would reduce the categories of dependants allowed to join families living in Britain. In January and February 1978, there was widespread media speculation about the details of the Conservative plans, and the 'race/immigration' theme again became the object of debate in the House of Commons. The Labour government pointed out, correctly, that stricter controls would involve breaking pledges already given and established in law and then made a series of desperate appeals for the issue not to be made a matter of further political debate. In the course of the intense media coverage, Home Secretary Merlyn Rees conceded in a television interview, on 5 February, that existing legislation was designed primarily to control 'coloured immigration'.

The Conservative Party's intentions were finally revealed on 7 April 1978 when a new nationality law was promised, along with new restrictions on the entry of dependants, husbands and fiancés. The party also promised a register of dependants from the Indian sub-continent and a quota system to regulate entry once the total number of registered dependants was known. These proposals took their place in the Conservative Party manifesto for the 1979 general election. They were given ideological significance when Margaret Thatcher said, on 17 April, that she stood by her statement made 15 months previously about the legitimacy of 'British people's fears' about 'being swamped'. In the election, the National Front vote collapsed and was collected by the Conservative Party.

The Conservative government of 1979–83 implemented most of its manifesto commitments and initiated a number of other policies – including a series of raids searching for 'illegal immigrants'. In the first six months of 1980, at least six raids were carried out by the police and immigration officers in Blackburn and London on Asian businesses; large numbers of employees, most of whom were not guilty of any offence, were questioned and arrested. In the past, warrants governing raids had named particular individuals who were being sought; the raids of 1980 were conducted using warrants which did not name suspected individuals. This was a policy that effectively required Asians and West Indians in Britain to carry their passports at all times. Collectively, these initiatives amounted to a new phase in the development of state racism.

A majority of the manifesto commitments were implemented with great speed. A White Paper containing proposed changes in the Immigration Rules was published on 14 November 1979 and was approved on 4 December. It contained a variety of new restrictions affecting, in particular, the parents, grand-parents and children aged over 18 of New Commonwealth migrants already in Britain, and husbands and fiancés of women living in Britain. The fact that the latter restrictions were not to apply to the wives and fiancées of men living in Britain, and that none of them applied to 'patrials' meant a further step in the direction of a 'white *man's* Britain'. Home Secretary Whitelaw denied that the new provisions were racist and sexist, but both the left and the right in the party argued, correctly, to the contrary.

Nigel Fisher, MP for Surbiton, followed a speech from the leader of the Liberal Party by saying: 'I agree . . . that my right Hon. Friend the Home Secretary cannot deny that his proposals discriminate against women and against race.' For the far right, Ronald Bell, MP for Beaconsfield, stated:

> I did not enter public life because I was bothered about the
> immigration of coloured people. Such a concept did not exist
> to any material degree in those days. But when the numbers
> increased in the late 1950s and early 1960s, any person who
> was not worried about it was neglecting his duty.

About those 'coloured people', he later claimed: 'Of course there is something genetically different about them.' For John Carlisle, MP for Luton west, these rules were regarded as the prelude to further restrictions which 'must unashamedly contain distinctions that are protective of our indigenous population. Only by such actions will the Government keep faith with the opinions of the vast majority of the people of this country.'

The strength and scale of openly racist opinion on the Conservative Back Benches was even more clearly revealed in a further debate on these new rules which was prompted by an Opposition motion on 10 March 1980. Harvey Proctor, MP for Basildon, argued that families could be reunited in 'their own countries' rather than Britain, and continued:

> Racial harmony and avoidance of strife will be achieved only when the indigenous population see a fall rather than a rise in the total New Commonwealth population resident in the United Kingdom. Simply stopping the immigrant flow will not now, regrettably, be sufficient to bring this about.

Consequently, he asked the Home Secretary to affirm 'that repatriation has a role to play for all those who wish to avail themselves of it.' Nick Budgen, MP for south-west Wolverhampton, contradicted the view of the Home Secretary: 'My Hon. Friend the Minister of State is being slightly less than frank with the House when he says that there is no racial discrimination in the proposals.' John Stokes, MP for Halesowen and Stourbridge, was explicit about the centrality of 'race': 'I do not fear civil strife, but I do fear that the England we know and love will be lost in a welter of new and different races, whose loyalty will still be to their original homeland, and whose customs will remain unchanged.' The most significant intervention was that by Tony Marlow, MP for north Northampton, who happily accepted the rules' racism on the grounds that racism was a 'natural' instinct:

> People have criticised these measures because they say they are racialist, as if racialist is a word of abuse. What does racialist mean? It means tribal. After all, man is a tribal animal. We have a feeling of kith and kin for people like ourselves, with our own background and culture.

The debate was largely between these far right MPs and the Labour Opposition, whose credibility was limited because of a previous Labour government's discrimination against the husbands and fiancés of women living in Britain.

On 30 July 1980, a White Paper on British Nationality Law was published. A draft Bill followed on 13 January 1981. The text confirmed that the government was primarily concerned to 'rationalise' the law on nationality in order to bring it into line with the system of immigration control based on 'patriality'. Thus, while the Immigration Acts of 1962 and 1968 had created first- and second-class UK citizens (depending upon your colour) the Nationality Bill (which became law later in the year) 'rationalised' the situation by taking away full citizenship from those already demoted to second class. The result was not one, but three classes of citizenship. The Labour Opposition gave the appearance of having returned to a position of principle. At the end of the second reading on the Bill, on 28 January, Roy Hattersley, MP for Sparkbrook, claimed that the Labour Party was opposing the Bill in the same spirit and with the same intentions as that of Gaitskell's opposition to the Commonwealth Immigrants Bill (1961). At the end of the debate on the third reading, on 4 June, he conceded that the Commonwealth Immigrants Act (1968) had been a serious mistake and committed a future Labour government to repeal of the British Nationality Act. But, with the successful passage of the Bill through parliament by the end of 1981, most of the Tories' manifesto commitments had been implemented. The register of dependants and the quota system were abandoned because of the large administrative costs and the complexity of the legislation such measures would require.

The implementation of most of the manifesto commitments was not enough to silence the far right, while failure to implement the others aroused their anger. Their campaign in favour of a policy of 'repatriation' continued. Powell repeated his arguments and demands at a meeting of Young Conservatives on 24 September 1981, in speeches to Havering Young Conservatives, on 7 November 1981, and to a Monday Club conference in May 1982. The Monday Club had been reactivated by a group of new Conservative MPs, and it quickly set up an Immigration and Repatriation Policy Committee, led by Harvey Proctor. A report of its deliberations appeared in October 1981, putting forward a plan to 'repatriate' 100,000 people of New Commonwealth 'ethnic origin' annually. In October 1982, Proctor spoke to another Monday Club policy statement which called for the setting up of a ministry for 'overseas resettlement' and for the abolition of the Commission for Racial Equality. These calls for 'repatriation' were given further endorsement in the pages of a new journal, the *Salisbury Review*, which aimed to provide a forum for the discussion of right-wing philosophy.

In an issue published in autumn 1982, an academic from Cambridge University, John Casey, suggested that the legal status of what he called the 'coloured immigrant community' (presumably including those born in Britain) be altered so that the people became 'guestworkers' who could be returned to their 'country of origin'. As part of the preamble to this suggestion, he described the West Indian population in Britain as being involved in 'a vastly disproportionate amount of violent crime'. The academic endorsement of a policy of 'repatriation' was continued by Professor John Vincent, of the University of Bristol, who wrote an article for the *Times*, on 10 November 1982. He called for a policy of 'assisted departures': 'It was a question of what public opinion saw, not of figures. The outflow of coloured emigrants was not enough to remove the justified fear of an increasing coloured population.'

The considerable strength of the far right wing of the Conservative Party was clearly demonstrated, and achieved massive publicity, in a political dispute which began in late 1982 over another redraft of the Immigration Rules. As had been widely predicted, the stricter racist and sexist Immigration Rules had become the subject of a complaint to the European Commission of Human Rights by five women who had been prevented from bringing their husbands to Britain because, as the rules laid down, they had not been born in Britain or did not have parents who were born in Britain. This pressure, along with the fact that the British Nationality Act itself required that certain changes be made, forced the government to amend the rules. Any such amendment would require a relaxation of the restrictions on the entry of foreign-born husbands and fiancés. As in the past, the right-wing press took the public initiative, predicting 'Tory fury' as it leaked the details of the proposed new rules before their publication on 25 October 1982. The right wing opposed the changes and supported a large group of Conservative Back Bench MPs, numbering over 50, who tabled an amendment opposing what they saw as an inevitable increase in migration and abuse of the arranged marriage system. There followed yet another moral panic about 'numbers' and 'alien culture', sustained by press reports in the *Daily Mail* and the *Daily Telegraph*, along with parliamentary questions, about alleged abuse of arranged marriages. Thus, the image of the West Indian 'mugger' was joined by the image of the 'wiley' Asian, willing to lie and forge documents in order to gain access to the 'honeypot'.

The government decided to amend the rules published on 25 October, despite the fact that abstention by the Labour Opposition ensured that they were not defeated at the end of the debate on 11 November. The amended rules imposed new conditions. Although all British women were to be allowed to bring in foreign-born fiancés and husbands, the entry-clearance officer had to be satisfied that the marriage was not one of convenience in order to allow the man to enter Britain, that the individuals planned to live together permanently, and that they had met. In addition, even if the entry-clearance officer was so satisfied, entry was granted initially for a two-year probation period. This did not satisfy the far right who objected to any increase in 'coloured immigration'. On 15 December, 18 Conservative MPs voted against the government and a further 28 abstained; combined with the opposition of the other parties, this guaranteed that the revised rules were defeated. A further set of rules was presented to the House of Commons and debated on 15 February, following a government decision to force the right wing to stop its opposition. These rules 'only' required the applicant to prove that the marriage was genuine. The government claimed that the operation of this condition for the first five weeks of 1983 had produced a refusal rate of 56 per cent from the Indian sub-continent. The fact that the rules had been so successful in reducing 'coloured immigration' was, along with political pressure, sufficient to reduce the number of rebels to 15. Although the far right eventually lost the vote, they had secured a major ideological victory by keeping the 'race/immigration' theme on the agenda of public and parliamentary debate from the middle of October 1982 to mid-February 1983.

There were two other events which, in different ways, were interpreted in terms which related to the 'race/immigration' theme. The first was the Falklands War of 1982, and its focusing on the notion of British national identity. This was how the prime minister expressed it on 3 July 1982:

> Now that it is all over, things cannot be the same again for we have learned something about ourselves – a lesson which we desperately need to learn. When we started out, there were the waverers and the fainthearts . . . There were those who would not admit it – even perhaps some here today – people who would have strenuously denied the suggestion but – in their heart of hearts – they too had their secret fears that it was true: that Britain was no longer the nation that had built an Empire and ruled a quarter of the world. Well they were wrong. The lesson of the Falklands is that Britain has not changed and that this nation still has those sterling qualities which shine through our history.

The reference to Britain as a 'nation' which built an Empire demonstrates the centrality of colonial exploitation to the political conception of national identity. Moreover, it is a conception of national identity which must, by definition, exclude all those who were the object of colonial exploitation – some of whose descendants now lived in Britain. John Casey returned to the point in the autumn 1982 issue of the *Salisbury Review*: 'the Falklanders were *British* . . . by language, custom and race.'

Naturally, migrants from the Caribbean and the Indian subcontinent and their children are excluded from this conception of British national identity. They have few grounds for finding glory in, for example, slavery and imperial domination – both of which have been justified by reference to the idea of 'race'. They would probably note the hostile language and imagery used about the 'Argies'; they would probably note its odd familiarity.

The second set of events were the riots which occurred in Bristol in April 1980 and throughout England in the summer of 1981. Political and ideological reaction extended over many months and combined a number of themes. The predominant government response was to condemn them as outbreaks of criminal behaviour which required a strong 'law and order' response from the police. To this was added the argument that the riots were a consequence of the declining authority and discipline on the part of parents and teachers. This 'law and order' theme was maintained against the widespread alternative interpretation which focused upon unemployment, material deprivation, police harassment and racism – and which underpinned the report by Lord Scarman on the Brixton riots in April 1981. But the far right saw something rather different.

Peregrine Worsthorne, writing in the *Sunday Times*, on 29 November 1981, defined Brixton as 'the iceberg tip of a crisis of ethnic criminality which is not Britain's fault – except in the sense that her rulers quite unnecessarily imported it – but the fault of the ethnic community itself, from whom the cure must come, as has the disease.' Within the Conservative Party itself, a similar process of criminalisation and racialisation occurred. In the debate on the third reading of the British Nationality Bill, on 4 June 1981, Harvey Proctor referred to 'mass migrations for three decades from the New Commonwealth and Pakistan and the dreadful and inevitable racial strife of which we see evidence weekly, if not yet daily, in metropolitan London and elsewhere.' Enoch Powell produced an even more apocalyptic prediction, on 16 July, when he referred to 'inner London becoming ungovernable or violence which could only effectively be described as civil war.' He concluded that it was the duty of the government to tell the electorate that one-third of the population of English cities would be 'coloured' before the end of the century.

The Conservative 1979–83 government therefore successfully tightened the system of racist immigration control and reproduced the 'race/immigration' theme as an important object of political debate. It explicitly justified this by arguing that 'our people's fears' are legitimate and must be acted upon. This is nothing other than a polite way of saying that racist policies and practices are required because 'our people' have racist opinions. Now it is certainly the case that racist views are widespread, but that is partly a product of political agitation and media publicity. This can be demonstrated by the results of an opinion poll, conducted in August and September 1981, amongst young people aged between 15 and 24 in two parts of

England. Published in the *Times* on 8 October 1981, the results showed: first, that 39 per cent of the sample believed that there were more than 10 million 'coloured people' in Britain, and a further 17 per cent believed that there were between 5 and 10 million. Thus, together, 56 per cent of the sample believed that there were more than 5 million 'coloured people' in Britain when, in reality, there are about 2.5 million. This is one crucial measure of the fact that 'our people's fears' are founded upon myth and rumour, and are mistaken. The major source of myth and rumour has been the continuing political agitation and media publicity about 'waves' of immigrants since the late 1950s (i.e. the period during which these interviewees grew up). Second, the sample was asked which of a range of suggested government policy options they supported regarding 'immigrants'. This shows that, although just under half (47 per cent) favoured a policy of 'equal treatment', almost the same proportion favoured a policy of either 'compulsory' (26 per cent) or 'voluntary repatriation' (18 per cent). The 'legitimate fears' of nearly half of 'our own young people' remain in favour of a policy of 'repatriation' despite the Conservative government's efforts to restrict 'coloured immigration' further. Clearly, 'our people's fears' have not yet been removed. Rather, the continuing political agitation around the 'race/immigration' theme has reproduced and perhaps even strengthened those 'fears'.

Conclusion

We regard the period since 1971 as a period characterised by a drift towards 'repatriation' because the 'fears' which have been referred to to justify government policy have been shown not to be satisfied solely by strict control over 'coloured immigration'. Strict control has existed since 1968 (all subsequent changes have been minor with the exception of the 1971 Immigration Act which increased the number of 'white' people free to enter Britain), while the 'race/immigration' theme has continually appeared as the object of political debate and media publicity. Moreover, even the state has admitted in this period that the system of immigration control is racist. In 1980, the Commission for Racial Equality attempted to carry out a formal investigation of the immigration service but the Home Office contested the legality of this in the High Court, during which its legal representative claimed:

> The whole of immigration control is based upon discrimination. It is of the essence of the Immigration Act that people will be discriminated against on the grounds of race or nationality and it is the function of certain officials to ensure that discrimination is effective.

There is now little that any government can do to limit 'coloured immigration' further, apart from preventing the entry of the remaining dependants of earlier migrants. Hence, those 'legitimate fears of being swamped' cannot be satisfied by racist immigration controls alone. Enoch Powell, in company with the neo-fascist groups, realised that a long time ago: a 'white man's Britain' can only be achieved by a policy of 'repatriation'. However, despite the drift in this direction, the events of this period have also shown that such a policy cannot be automatically set in motion, even by a right-wing government. There are a number of reasons for this.

First, a belief in the principle of equal treatment for all British citizens is held by important sections of the political ruling class. It does not follow that this principle will always be realised but its continuing expression provides a measure of the adequacy of state policy and practice. It is for this reason that successive governments have consistently denied that their immigration legislation has been racist and sexist. Such a denial would not be so easy in the case of an active, state policy of 'repatriation' of New Commonwealth migrants and their British-born children. Moreover, the fact that immigration control affects people at the point of entry means that the effects are, in an important sense, hidden from domestic view. This would not be so with a policy of 'repatriation'. Second, the migrants (now settlers) have continued to provide labour power to key sectors of the economy, sectors often, but not exclusively, characterised by manual, low-skill labour, low wages, shift work, etc. (see chapter 6). A policy of repatriation requires that 'indigenous labour' is willing, or can be forced, to enter these positions. Third, a policy of 'repatriation' would meet with the active opposition of the migrants themselves, and would require considerable force to implement.

Nevertheless, the repeated claim by the Conservative government that it is committed in principle to the equal treatment of all British citizens cannot be taken too seriously. After all, in the mid-1950s, it was a matter of principle that an Indian or a Jamaican could believe that he or she was a British citizen and could settle in Britain. In the early 1960s, it was a matter of principle that anyone holding a UK passport was guaranteed entry into Britain. There was a retreat from these principles, why not from others? What is at issue is not whether such a retreat is possible but, given the history we have outlined, under what conditions would it be possible?

At the most general level, we believe the conditions are as follows. First, there has to be a continuing and increasing political agitation for 'repatriation' – agitation that is itself dependent upon a growing common-sense belief that the presence of the migrants and their children is problematic. Second, there must be a declining need for the labour power of the migrants and their children, or an alternative source of supply. Third, the government would have to be willing and able to deal with the international pressures that would follow from a policy which would involve stripping a section of the population of its British citizenship. Fourth, the government would have to be sufficiently authoritarian to deal with the resistance of those directly affected by the policy, as well as those who would object to such a racist and authoritarian measure.

At first sight, these might appear to be 'exceptional' conditions. However, the economic and political crisis of British capitalism that has unfolded since the early 1970s may produce them. The Conservative governments elected in 1979 and 1983 have decisively broken with the post-1945 political and ideological consensus, and fostered an ideology whose roots have a distinctly authoritarian pedigree. The government's attempt to restructure British capitalism has led to massive unemployment. This constitutes an economic foundation for a policy of 'repatriation'. Unemployment has now reached the point where those whose labour power was so urgently required in the 1950s are no longer necessary. Moreover, there are now considerable economic and political pressures upon the unemployed to move into the remaining low-pay and low-skill sectors of the economy that were earlier filled by migrants. At the political level, it is clear that the government is willing to endorse authoritarian measures: its support for the police and its trade union legislation illustrate this. And, ideologically, we have witnessed the developing racialisation and criminalisation of West Indian and Asian people in Britain by the police, media and by a growing group of Conservative politicians.

In these 'exceptional' conditions, there is a crucial relationship between political context, the politics of the leadership of the government and the strength of the far right wing of the Conservative Party. The fact that two Conservative candidates in the 1983 general election had a history of activism in neo-fascist politics is evidence of the extent to which the move to the right by the leadership has made the party an attractive location for neo-fascists. Right-wing Back Bench pressure will be effective when the leadership publicly expresses views and policies which were previously confined to those same Back Benches. Furthermore, political agitation within the Conservative Party in favour of 'repatriation' has increased in a period when the resistance to racism (including state racism) has also increased. The fact of resistance, which shows every sign of continuing, has been consistently appropriated by the far right to support their argument about the inevitability of 'racial' conflict.

5. Racism, fascism and the state

Introduction

The political significance of neo-fascist political organisations was limited until the late 1960s, although one should not ignore the local effects of their activities before then, particularly in the attacks on West Indians in London in 1958. Since the late 1960s, however, and especially after 1973, a number of neo-fascist parties have attracted a certain degree of political support and have considerably influenced parliamentary politics. More recently, their activities have led, directly and indirectly, to the deaths of more and more West Indian and Asian people as racist violence has spread throughout the country. This growing influence of neo-fascism in Britain is not the product of outside intervention or of the activities of an isolated lunatic fringe. Neo-fascist politics began to attract support when the Conservative government proved unwilling to put into practice its election commitment to 'strict immigration control'. The decision to admit a large proportion of the Asians expelled from Uganda created the political space for a more extreme political organisation. In other words, there is a direct relationship between racism, fascism and the British state. Although the British state is still a long way from embracing fascism, it is the case that the development of state racism has helped prepare the ground for the emergence of neo-fascism as a political force in Britain.

Neo-fascism in Britain since 1950

The Second World War, widely understood as a war against fascism, helped to destroy almost all support for fascist politics in Britain. In the 1930s, such support as there had been was not widespread: fascism had never become a mass, popular movement in Britain. In the early 1950s, therefore, fascist activity amounted to little more than an attempt by a small group of individuals to create an appropriate political vehicle by which to propagate their political ideas. The most significant was the League of Empire Loyalists (LEL), formed in 1954 by A.K. Chesterton whose personal politics can be best summarised as a combination of anti-semitism, anti-communism and anti-Americanism. The LEL was primarily a pressure group, whose objective was to restore to the Conservative Party some of its supposedly forgotten ideals and principles. In this respect, the LEL largely failed. It did, however, provide a training ground for a group of individuals who, subsequently, figured prominently in the history of neo-fascism in Britain.

The mob attacks upon West Indian migrants and their property in Nottingham and London in 1958 provided a context for many of these individuals to declare their political ideas more explicitly. The National Labour Party (NLP) had been active in Notting Hill since June and its propaganda played a part in encouraging and justifying the attacks. An organisation called the White Defence League (WDL) was also very active in Notting Hill from the summer of 1958 onwards. Both organisations propagated a racist message which was linked to more far-ranging fascist principles. On 15 June 1959, Colin Jordan, leader of the WDL, was quoted in the *Daily Herald*: 'If a Fascist is a person who wants to keep Britain white, then I am a Fascist and proud of it.'

In common with Cyril Osborne, these organisations wanted a 'white man's Britain'; they also wanted more than that. Whereas Osborne was committed to parliamentary democracy, Jordan and company wanted an authoritarian state modelled on the German Nazi example. But they agreed on the need to racialise British politics, though the neo-fascists hoped that, once this had been achieved, they would be able to outflank the Conservative Party in appealing to those who had come to support the idea of a 'white man's Britain'. This was not to happen. Although the neo-fascists continued their propaganda activities, their membership figures remained tiny.

The history of the next nine years is one of organisational splits and reorganisation amongst the small group of neo-fascists whose only high spot each year was the celebration of Hitler's birthday. In 1960, the NLP and the WDL merged to form the British National Party (BNP). This small organisation split in 1962 on the question of whether or not to present itself publicly as a fascist party, those in favour leaving to form the National Socialist Movement (NSM). The latter devoted much of its energy to the formation of a paramilitary organisation, complete with full Nazi regalia. 'Military manoeuvres' and camp-fire songs extolling the virtues of the British 'race' eventually led to the imprisonment of four of its leaders, including Colin Jordan and John Tyndall. In the same period, another individual who later become politically prominent, Martin Webster, published an article called 'Why I am a Nazi'. Disillusioned with the fact that, despite the wide publicity they achieved as a result of the trials, the British people seemed uninterested in such clear statements of principle, the NSM split; another organisation was born, the Greater Britain Movement (GBM). The leadership of the GBM, including John Tyndall, made an attempt to dissociate itself from fascist symbols and propaganda, leaving the NSM as the only organisation clearly professing its fascist credentials. But the idea of 'race' remained prominent. Part of the GBM's programme stated:

> For the protection of British blood, racial laws will be enacted
> forbidding marriage between Britons and non-Aryans.
> Medical measures will be taken to prevent procreation on the
> part of all those who have hereditary defects, whether racial,
> mental or physical. A pure, strong, healthy British race will
> be regarded as the principal guarantee of Britain's future.

However, the change of public image brought no greater success: the GBM's total membership did not exceed 138 people. By 1967, the neo-fascist organisations' main achievement was the conviction of their leaders on charges of assault, possession of firearms and the organisation of a paramilitary force. To them, 'destiny' must have seemed very cruel. Their failure was due not least to the fact that they were not the only people anxious to keep 'coloured immigrants' out of Britain: the Labour and Conservative parties were competing to prove each more able than the other to do that.

Political failure and organisational fragmentation were the main factors which led to A.K.Chesterton's formation of the National Front (NF) in 1967. The NF incorporated the membership of three organisations – the LEL, the BNP and the

Racial Preservation Society (RPS). The aim was to provide a new arena for far-right activism, outside the Conservative Party and as an independent political organisation. A clear commitment to parliamentary democracy was declared and a combination of nationalist policies was formulated. These included opposition to entry to the European Economic Community, a strengthening of 'law and order', a 'reconstruction' of the Empire, and compulsory repatriation of all 'coloured immigrants'. The NF combined the experience of many far-right activists with a clear set of political objectives; those excluded from the organisation were alarmed that they might be bypassed by events. They immediately began a campaign to join the NF and, to this end, the GBM was dissolved. The desire for political unity in the context of shared political assumptions and the clever application of pressure led, first, to their membership and, second, to their taking control of the NF. By the end of the decade, the NF was firmly in the hands of those whose public commitment to fascism in the 1960s had led them to court and to jail.

Despite this fact, the NF presented itself and its policies in a different light. Its leadership dismissed their previous political allegiances as 'youthful indiscretion'. As apparent proof of its commitment to the parliamentary process, the NF fielded ten candidates in the 1970 general election. It achieved little success. Collectively, the candidates obtained 3.6 per cent of the vote, their best performance being 5.6 per cent in a London constituency. In this period, the NF also sought to infiltrate the right-wing Monday Club. The Monday Club had been formed in 1961 and provided a forum for radical right-wing individuals and Conservative MPs. Particularly concerned with Britain's withdrawal from Empire in Africa and with 'coloured immigration' to Britain, it had attracted both publicity and members after Powell's speeches in 1968. By 1972, it claimed the support of 34 Conservative MPs (including Ronald Bell and John Stokes) and 2,000 national members. It committed itself to 'voluntary repatriation', among other right-wing policies, which it hoped to pressure the Conservative Party into accepting. The Monday Club's post-Powell expansion put it in direct competition with the NF. The NF's strategy of infiltration aimed to win over its support and, ultimately, destroy it. This achieved further notoriety for the NF, as did co-operation at local level between NF and Monday Club members. But notoriety was not translated into wider political support.

It was not until late 1972 that the NF's fortunes began to change. Following the Conservative government's decision on the Ugandan Asians, the NF mounted a picket at Heathrow Airport. In return, they obtained public support and media attention. By 1973, the NF was reported to have 14,000 members, and, in a by-election in West Bromwich in May 1973, it obtained 16 per cent of the vote.

The sudden general election in February 1974 must have suggested that destiny at last smiled on the NF; the organisation responded by fielding 54 candidates. It was a major organisational and financial effort – especially in lost deposits, as the average vote for each candidate was only 3.2 per cent. However, the shift from political obscurity to media attention, along with an increasing membership, intimated a more positive future than that suggested by the election result alone. A decision to hold a national demonstration in London, in June 1974, increased media interest – especially after a left-wing organisation, Liberation, called a counter-demonstration. The police defended the NF's 'right' to the free expression of racism; the resulting confrontation between anti-fascists and the police – in the course of which one demonstrator was killed – meant further exposure for the NF. The second general election of the year, in October, provided another opportunity for the NF to test its electoral support. On this occasion, 94 constituencies were contested and the NF candidates polled an average of 3.1. per cent of the vote.

This was no great breakthrough. Moreover, membership declined to around 9,000 members. The resulting internal wrangle over strategy and organisation led to a split in 1976 and the formation of the short-lived National Party (NP). Still, for the NF, destiny smiled once more. In the same year, a small number of Malawi Asians arrived in Britain, a Sikh boy was murdered in Southhall and Robert Relf was jailed for an offence against the Race Relations Act. On the crest of the resulting moral panic about 'race/immigration', the NF reaped an electoral reward in the local elections in 1976 and 1977. In these two years, the NF obtained over 10 per cent of the vote in 25 districts; in two, it won just over 20 per cent. There were more political demonstrations and meetings, which the NF held in areas populated by a significant proportion of New Commonwealth migrants and their children. For the NF, these marches were symbolic acts of 'territorial reoccupation'.

All this was interpreted to mean that the NF was rapidly gaining political support and was on the road to power. There was a grassroots mobilisation in the areas where NF demonstrations were held. The police continued to allow the NF to march, a policy which led to running battles with anti-fascist demonstrators – the largest being in Lewisham, London, in 1977. Opposition to the NF was organised in the form of the Anti-Nazi League and, as we have seen, voiced by both the Labour Party and the TUC.

The 1979 general election set the scene for a major test of organisational and ideological strength. The NF proudly announced its intention of fielding 303 candidates and talked confidently of forming a government. The result was a disaster. All the candidates lost their deposits and, collectively, they obtained just 1.3 per cent of the vote. The NF's failure to make any sort of electoral breakthrough was obvious to all. There followed a major re-evaluation of strategy which soon degenerated into an open conflict over both politics and personalities.

The immediate outcome was the disintegration of the NF into a number of small splinter groups. Much effort went into factional attacks and, later, tentative moves towards reorganisation. The NF continued to exist, led by Martin Webster who managed to keep himself in the national news as a result of various legal charges against him. Many of the other NF leaders and members were involved in the formation of the British National Party (BNP) in April 1982. The organisation which had threatened to eclipse the National Front after the 1979 general election, the British Movement (BM), was, by 1982, in decline, facing large debts and lacking any coherent national organisation. In addition, at the end of 1982, there were a number of very small organisations active in various parts of the country, including the National Socialist Action Party, the National Socialist Workers' Initiative and the World Union of National Socialists. Although these various organisations are still involved in sectarian rivalry, they have in common an open commitment to fascist ideology and propaganda work which focuses upon the idea of 'race' and the demand for 'compulsory repatriation'. Moreover, although prepared to fight elections for publicity purposes, they no longer make any pretence of gaining power by electoral means. They are now more openly involved in political violence and, in some cases, paramilitary organisation.

Neo-fascism and political violence

The historical account of neo-fascism in Britain since 1950 implies that, after the formation of the NF in 1967, the political activity of neo-fascists was limited to electoral competition. Although the electoral strategy was predominant, this did not prevent the use of political violence, although, up until 1979, much of it was initiated at the local rather than the national level. Thus, for example, in September 1974, some 50 members of the NF forced the Home Secretary to abandon a speech in Chichester Cathedral. In November 1975, a group of NF members broke up a National Council for Civil Liberties meeting at the University of Manchester, as a result of which many of those in attendance ended up in hospital. In February 1978, two NF members were convicted of planning the physical harassment of Asians. And, in the late 1970s, there were two court cases involving charges against NF members for possessing bomb-making equipment. In addition, one writer who got to know a section of the NF membership well identified a 'culture of violence' within the organisation which encouraged physical violence against political opponents, West Indians and Asians.

Electoral failure in 1979 was followed by organised and escalating violence. Soon after the election, the NF found itself outflanked by the British Movement, a descendant of the National Socialist Movement of the 1960s. The NSM had rejected the 'respectable' strategy of electoral intervention and had maintained its open identification with fascism. Confined to almost total obscurity throughout the 1970s, the NSM, renamed the BM, emerged 'untainted' by electoral deviation after the NF's electoral disaster. The BM set about recruiting a new generation of working-class skinheads, well known for their male machismo and racist beliefs. Some responded positively to calls for direct action and the use of swastika armbands and Nazi salutes. Aggressive demonstrations and physical attacks on Asians, West Indians and left-wingers followed.

This shift from electoral to 'street politics' intensified the internal disputes within the NF, and one faction set about following the BM's example. From 1980, physical attacks on West Indians and Asians, and arson attacks on their property, dramatically increased. Some Asians and West Indians were murdered. Britain's right-wing press was more interested in defining the 'law and order' problem in terms of 'black crime' and devoted little attention to fascist violence. The evidence was soon so extensive and detailed that the Home Office was forced to conduct its own investigation in 1980–1.

Its report was published in 1981. It confirmed that there had been a dramatic rise in racist attacks and that they were now widespread, and that neo-fascist propaganda 'is a crucial element in creating the climate in which a minority of people find it fashionable to engage in overt displays of violent racialism, or overt displays which could lead to racial conflict.' However, having refused to consider evidence submitted by the anti-fascist journal *Searchlight*, it denied that neo-fascist organisations had conspired to organise these attacks. This is contradicted by the evidence of successful prosecutions in British courts against persons who are members of the BM or NF, or who have admitted in court to be sympathisers. In 1980, 14 such persons were convicted for attacks on West Indians and Asians, or for possessing bomb-making equipment. In 1981, 38 members or sympathisers were convicted of similar offences.

There is no doubt that the increase in racist attacks and murders in the 1980s has been a result of a strategic decision by the neo-fascists. The electoral failure of the NF and the move to the right within the Conservative Party, in a context of continuing economic crisis, have persuaded neo-fascist leaders that a collapse of parliamentary democracy is possible. Their role in this is to encourage social conflict and street violence.

Ideology and political support

The events of the early 1980s show that there is no ambiguity about the political ideology of the NF and other organisations.

However, this is not the case for the 1970s, when the NF denied that it was a fascist party and claimed a commitment to parliamentary democracy. Some writers have taken these claims at face value and concluded that the ideology of the NF was no more than an extreme form of conservative nationalism. It is true that extreme nationalism is a central element of the NF's political ideology. For the NF, and other groups, nationalism is regarded as a 'natural' expression of the British 'race' which is 'naturally' antagonistic towards other 'races', including those which are considered to be biologically inferior. Consequently, the ideas of 'race' and 'nation' overlap to a considerable extent in NF ideology. This racist nationalism leads logically to the policy of 'compulsory repatriation'. But there was more to NF political ideology than this. Although the NF's campaign was built around this conservative nationalism, its internal literature and political education was rather different. It is the latter which shows the NF's racist nationalism to be derived from a more general fascist ideology.

The main link between the ideology of the NF leadership and that of the German Nazis is found in the fiction of the 'Jewish world conspiracy', a fiction which has its roots in forged documents, the *Protocols of the Elders of Zion*. This document purports to record a meeting of 'World Jewry', in the early twentieth century, which formulated a plan to set up an international government and take control of the world. This alleged Jewish conspiracy is said to be so successful that it now controls both the American and Russian governments. One of the means of weakening nationalist sentiment and control is to encourage 'race mixing', which is believed to lead to biological degeneration. In the case of Britain, the suggestion is that Jewish conspirators and British governments have colluded to promote immigration from the New Commonwealth for this purpose. Additionally, one can find in this same literature a commitment to what is variously defined as a government of 'strength' and 'determination' or, more explicitly, as a government which would not betray nation and 'race'. These are major qualifications to the concept of parliamentary democracy, and reminiscent of the publicly declared authoritarianism of the 1950s and 1960s.

Thus, throughout the 1970s, the political ideology of the NF did contain central elements of the fascist tradition. Though not publicly expressed, they provided the political foundation for the manifestos and propaganda distributed through the 1970s. This helps us to understand the regular warning of the NF leadership that, although racism may have been an important avenue by which individuals could be attracted to the organisation, it did not, in itself, go far enough. Before returning to the significance of this point, we will show the main features of political success that the NF achieved with this strategy and propaganda.

The local and national election results achieved by the NF rise from a low point in 1970 to a peak in 1976–7 and decline thereafter. Membership figures tell a similar story, although in this case the peak was in 1973–4, when the total stood at 14,000; thereafter it declined to about 7,000 for the rest of the 1970s. But support was not evenly spread across Britain. It was concentrated in certain areas of working-class residence in England's major industrial towns and cities as well as in a number of seaside towns, especially on the south coast. The latter shows that one source of support for the NF was from retired or elderly Conservative Party supporters who believed that the party has 'gone soft', particularly on the 'immigration question'. The former shows that a proportion of working-class voters were willing to vote for the NF.

The urban areas where the NF gained support in the 1970s were of two kinds. They were either areas of long-established industrial production which had been recently experiencing the effects of cyclical decline, or they were new areas of post-1945 capitalist expansion which, by the 1970s, had stopped expanding and were showing signs of crisis. In the former, industrial decline compounded the problems arising from a long-term shortage of housing and more general social decay. Migrant labour had been attracted into both types of area in the 1950s and 1960s, either as replacement labour (to occupy the places vacated by workers who were searching for cleaner jobs with higher rates of pay), or as the only source of labour for new and expanding sectors of capital. However, as we argued in chapter 2, with the onset of decline in these areas, the Asian and West Indian workers became the scapegoats. The idea of 'race' came to have a great deal of local, common-sense significance. For a minority, the political debate between the Labour and Conservative parties about 'strict immigration control', followed by the Conservative 'betrayal' over the Ugandan Asians, offered nothing in the way of an immediate solution to the real, material problems as they experienced them. Having identified 'the coloureds' as the cause of the problems they faced, therein they also found the solution. Disillusion with both the Labour and Conservative parties was therefore followed by support for the NF, a party which promised not just 'strict immigration control', but 'compulsory repatriation'.

Working-class electoral support for the NF in these areas was a product of that organisation's more extreme racialisation of domestic politics. But the support was not necessarily permanent. First, it soon became clear that the NF could not deliver the goods: without political power, 'compulsory repatriation' was no more than a promise, and promises did not solve the material problems. Second, by the late 1970s, the various anti-NF campaigns had successfully exposed the NF's fascist pedigree. This was sufficient to persuade at least a proportion of NF voters to seek an alternative for their racist-inspired vote. Hence, although the NF was a vehicle for the mobilisation and expression of racism amongst sections of the English working class, it failed to translate this into permanent and more generalised support for neo-fascist politics. We should not conclude from this that the influence of the NF was therefore negligible. Another dimension of the history of the NF suggests otherwise.

State racism and neo-fascism

The NF obtained little political support before 1973. Its electoral support slumped in the general election of 1979. The NF's breakthrough came after the admission to Britain of a proportion of the Asians expelled from Uganda, while the decline in its electoral support occurred in the context of the election of a right-wing Conservative government which, in the period preceding the election, had emphasised its commitment to 'strict immigration control'. This served to attract previous NF voters who were anxious that something be done to improve their circumstances immediately. There is clearly a relationship here between political support for neo-fascism and the consistency with which the state implements its racist strategy.

The system of immigration control established by Conservative and Labour governments was designed to keep out 'coloured immigrants'. Their justification was that it would satisfy 'public opinion' (that is, racist pressures). In fact, it has had the opposite effect: it has raised expectations of even stricter legislation to 'keep the blacks out', even to 'send them back home'. Hence, the Conservative government's decision over the Ugandan Asians was, for racist opinion, a great betrayal, and the political initiative passed partially from the state to the NF. From 1973 to 1979, NF activity focused political attention on 'the blacks' and on the demand for 'compulsory repatriation'. Since 1979, the various neo-fascist groups have continued their racialisation of British politics by their involvement in racist violence and murder. For these reasons, the political impact of the NF has been much greater than the electoral evidence by itself suggests; the precondition for that impact was the racialisation of British politics by Labour and Conservative governments, and by Enoch Powell. Their decisions had defined the problem as one of 'race/immigration' but, so far, only the neo-fascists have been prepared to be explicit about the logical solution, 'compulsory repatriation'.

The fact that the Conservative Party was able to steal its electoral support forced the NF (and other neo-fascist groups) to change their strategy. As the Conservative Party has moved to the right, the neo-fascists have moved further to the right. Hence, they have rejected 'electoral respectability' and returned to street politics. But they are nevertheless eager to retain links with the Conservative Party; there are also elements in the Conservative Party who wish to retain direct contact with the neo-fascists. This interrelationship is evident in a number of forms. Some individuals previously active in neo-fascist politics have joined the Conservative Party and have been selected as parliamentary candidates. For example, the unsuccessful Conservative candidate for Stockton south in the 1983 general election was Thomas Finnegan. His previous political career included holding the positions of secretary of the Birmingham NF and west Midlands organiser of the NF. He twice stood as a NF parliamentary candidate in 1974 in the Erdington constituency. The journal *Searchlight* has traced links between four other Conservative Party candidates in June 1983 (all of whom were elected) and extremist right-wing groups. Further evidence of this interrelationship is found in the activities of various co-ordinating groups, ostensibly concerned with immigration control and 'repatriation'. These provide a meeting-place for neo-fascists and the far right of the Conservative Party. The Young Conservative's National Advisory Committee, which has become increasingly concerned about neo-fascist infiltration of the Conservative Party, has investigated these groups, amongst other links. Its report, in draft form, was leaked to the national press just before the Conservative Party annual conference in October 1983. The *Times*, on 10 October, printed extracts from the draft report which draws the following conclusions:

> It is our considered opinion that a number of Conservative
> MPs are too closely connected with the extremist co-
> ordinating groups . . . The tendency for certain MPs to share
> platforms with people and groups whose views are wholly
> inconsistent with the Tory Party is extremely disturbing . . .
> We are led to the conclusion that extremist and racialist forces
> are at work inside the Conservative Party.

The close relationship between state racism and neo-fascism has raised a major issue for those involved in the struggle against racism and fascism. The Anti-Nazi League was able to help organise and lead that struggle in 1978 and 1979, but its propaganda and activity focused upon the NF. It had success in establishing a connection between the NF and the German Nazi party, but this could not have had any major impact upon the underlying nature and extent of racist belief. It did break the emerging link between racist opinion and a particular neo-fascist organisation, but the main force behind racism in Britain since the late 1950s has been the state. The successful labelling of the NF as a neo-fascist party helped to neutralise the political impact of the NF, but the 1979 election result demonstrated that racism continued to be an important political force.

Racism, neo-fascism and capitalist crisis

The failure of the left to confront the role of the state in the maintenance of racism was matched by the failure of the NF to generate an organised fascist movement in the 1970s. In 1969, John Tyndall, an NF leader, claimed:

> Nothing is more depressing than meeting, as one often does these days, people whose political outlook starts and finishes with an embittered sourness towards immigrants. No serious movement in politics can ever function on a sentiment such as this.

At the annual general meeting of the NF in 1976, he made the same point in a different way:

> Let us remember that only certain areas are touched by immigration. Let us also remember that on the questions of the economy the British electorate does not consist of experts or specialists; it is difficult for them as ordinary men and women to sort out one economic argument from another. But there is one thing that the great majority of the electorate can immediately recognise – and they recognise it by instinct rather than by any form of intellectual understanding: that is, a party which has the strength and the will to govern and to rule.

In both cases, Tyndall was arguing that although racism may be an important means by which people approach the politics of the NF, the party could not achieve anything politically by simply mobilising racist sentiment. The aim of, and problem for, the NF was to generate a fascist ideology amongst its supporters and to convince the electorate that it had the will and capacity to constitute a 'strong' government, strong enough to carry through 'compulsory repatriation' along with a series of other authoritarian measures. The membership and electoral statistics show that the NF failed in both respects. The origin of the problem lies in the fact that, for historical reasons, racism is an important component of the political consciousness of all classes in Britain. It had already been successfully mobilised before the NF was formed. The other side of the success of the NF in capturing some of this racist sentiment was the demonstration that it did not automatically translate into a broader, fascist ideology. This raises the question of the relationship between fascism and racism.

Fascism refers to an ideology and political strategy which, if successful, leads to a certain form of political domination. It accepts the capitalist economy but desires national political and economic reorganisation in order to achieve national economic success. The ideology is authoritarian and nationalist and accentuates the need for a strong state in order to carry through its political and economic objectives. This usually means the abolition of all other political parties and of the wide range of political freedoms that have accompanied the rise of parliamentary democracy in western Europe, freedoms that have been achieved as a result of mass political struggle. Consequently, one of the aims of the fascist parties is the elimination of independent working-class political and trade-union organisation. All this amounts to a revolution within a capitalist society engineered from the right – a revolution which retains capitalism, but fundamentally alters the political and ideological terms on which capitalism survives. The strategy for achieving this includes the development of a mass political movement, mobilising in particular the 'middle class' by means of nationalist sentiment and the widespread use of violence and terror against its identified opponents. What becomes crucial is whether or not a large section of the capitalist class concludes that fascism alone offers the possibility of maintaining and improving their economic circumstances. This presumes an economic crisis of significant proportions, the political solution to which is then conceived of in radical, right-wing terms.

Racism is not necessarily a prominent element in this ideology and political strategy, as the history of fascism in Italy and Spain demonstrates. However, it is an ever-present possibility because of the centrality of nationalism to the fascist solution to economic crisis. The nationalist argument will always assert that there is a particular population which is bound together by a common history and culture. It is this distinctiveness which constitutes the boundary of this supposed nation. This ideology of nationalism, however, originated in the same period as the 'scientific' formulation of racism and shares with it the idea of a naturally constituted population, identifiable in terms of its culture. Racism goes one step further in asserting that cultural distinctiveness and hierarchy are grounded in biological difference. Hence, whether or not nationalism is expressed through the idea of 'race' will depend upon historical circumstances.

In Britain, nationalism is expressed by means of the idea of 'race' because the object of national identity revolves around its history of relations with other peoples, reflecting the fact of Britain's rise to industrial and military supremacy as the first, fully developed capitalist society. The history of those relations is a history of war in Europe and beyond, including the Empire. Both the populations with whom conflict occurred, and the fact of conflict itself, were understood by the nineteenth century in terms of the idea of 'race'. The importance of war and colonialism – allied to the notion of 'kith and kin' – to the definition of British national identity was clearly exposed in the course of the conflict over the Falkland Islands in 1982. But these same factors have been exposed in the course of the political conflicts that developed over the migration of labour from the New Commonwealth in the 1950s and 1960s. Right-wing nationalists (and that term now includes the leadership of the Conservative Party) have consistently defined the migrants and their children as the 'enemy within', as 'alien stock' which threatens the survival of the British people and British culture.

The overlap between the ideas of 'race' and 'nation' is to some extent shared across the parliamentary political spectrum. The position adopted by the leadership of the Labour Party on the conflict over the Falkland Islands is evidence of that. But it is only on the Conservative right, and beyond, that the ideas become synonymous and directly expressed in some notion of biological difference. Given this conception of British national identity, it is no surprise that neo-fascist movements should have had some success in mobilising support using notions which express both nationalism and racism. This constitutes ideological common ground with the right wing of the Conservative Party. But the neo-fascists have the task of translating the support that they receive as a result of their propaganda for 'compulsory repatriation' into support for an authoritarian, fascist state. What happened in the 1930s and the 1970s shows that it is relatively easy in circumstances of economic and political crisis for fascists to mobilise sections of the working class (including its non-manual fractions) and the petit-bourgeoisie by means of racism, but much more difficult to transform this into a fascist mass movement. One of the most important reasons for this in the 1970s was the role of the state in both practising and legitimating racism. As long as the state can retain the initiative in this matter, the opportunities for the neo-fascists will be limited.

In this context, it is no accident that the years of greatest neo-fascist success (1974–9) were those in which the state was formally controlled by a weak, vacillating Labour government and during which the Conservative Party was undergoing an ideological shift to the right following the failure of the Heath government of 1970–4. The Labour government failed to deal with the political and economic crisis of capitalism and ended up implementing policies which set a precedent for the future Conservative government. A dimension of the political crisis came to focus on the 'race/immigration' theme, partly because of the half-hearted attempts to soften the impact of racist immigration controls. The electoral success of the right-wing Conservative Party in 1979 and 1983 shows that the electoral ground captured by the neo-fascists in the mid-1970s can be recaptured by a party of the right. The current reality is that the economic and political crisis of capitalism is being contained within the framework of an increasingly authoritarian state which, nevertheless, retains the existing parliamentary structures.

However, the way in which the crisis is being contained reproduces the conditions for the survival of the neo-fascists. The Conservative government's legislation on immigration control and nationality continue the ideological tradition which goes back to 1961, while many of its other policies, both domestic and international, are framed within, and express, an explicit, right-wing nationalism. More specifically, the government has so far refused to curb the growth of neo-fascist-inspired violence and murder. In such circumstances, what becomes crucial is not so much whether the neo-fascists can resolve their sectarian disputes (although this is a necessary condition), but whether the Conservative government can continue to contain the economic and political crisis. There is little evidence that the underlying condition of the British economy will improve (although British capital, both manufacturing and finance, which is operating outside Britain is experiencing more success) and so the possibility of the right-wing Conservative government retaining the political initiative is problematic. A split in the Conservative government, a parliament without a majority government, or another vacillating Labour government are all circumstances that would then open the door to the possibility of new neo-fascist success.

Conclusion

State racism and the growth of neo-fascism in Britain since the 1960s are inseparable. For this reason, the possibility of the implementation of the major, remaining racist demand, 'repatriation', remains real. The racialisation of British politics is being continued both by government policy and ideology, and by neo-fascist violence. It is conceivable that a political crisis arising out of a combination of the growing resistance to racism and fascist-inspired violence would push a right-wing government to take the 'repatriation' option – although in a weak form in the first instance. Some will argue that this is impossible because the government has committed itself in principle to the equal treatment of all British citizens and is, in any case, not motivated by racism.

These arguments are not persuasive. First, the history of the institutionalisation of racism by the state in Britain is a history of a retreat from principle. There is now a large number of Conservative MPs prepared to argue that West Indian and Asian people in Britain are not really British in terms of 'culture' and 'stock' – an argument that could be used to justify a decision by the government that they are no longer entitled to British citizenship. Second, it is of little relevance whether or not particular government ministers are directly motivated by racism in some deep personal sense. The fact is that both Labour and Conservative governments have opted for racist solutions in particular situations; justifications for these solutions are increasingly dominated by reference to the 'legitimate fears of our people'. This is a justification which endorses racist ideas and which could equally well be used to support a policy of 'repatriation'. In the current period the main influence of the neo-fascists is to assist the creation of social conflict and disorder. This conflict could well help to persuade the government that a further concession to 'our people's fears' is necessary to ensure its political survival.

6. The migration of labour and capital: the global context

We now shift our attention to the connections between the racialisation of British domestic politics and the migration of labour and capital, both historically and on a world scale. The development of the ideology of racism is closely connected with the large-scale movements of population from one geographical area to another, movements which originate in the emergence and development of capitalism. But it is not only people who are forced to migrate by material conditions. Capital, too, is moved from one geographical location to another in the search for the best conditions to realise profit and to further the expansion of the capitalist system.

The emphasis in the preceding chapters has been upon political and ideological processes; it is now on economic relations. However, these different levels of determination and effect are not so isolated from each other. Economic factors were implicated in the process of racialisation, and political and ideological factors play a part in the migration of labour and capital. But these are not equal determinations and effects. It is the very nature of capitalism as a mode of production, as a method of 'satisfying' the material and cultural needs of human life, which sets definite limits to the influence of political and ideological factors. Hence, although the ideology of racism has an origin in pre-capitalist relations, and has its own independent effects within capitalism, it has been the rise of capitalist relations of production which has provided the context for, and set limits to, the major influence of racism since the middle of the seventeenth century. In a type of society in which everything (including labour power) becomes a commodity, an object of exchange to realise profit, racism is one form of ideology which has a particular power both to structure and justify the particular patterns of exploitation that have emerged historically. The emergence of these problems is grounded in the migration of labour and capital.

Hence, in this chapter, we explain, first, why migrants came from the New Commonwealth to Britain in the 1950s and 1960s. Second, we show that this particular migration represents a new phase of labour migration which can be traced back into European history and which has been associated with prior expressions of racism. Third, we show how the migration of labour to Britain in the 1950s and 1960s was part of a wider process that occurred throughout Western Europe. Finally, we argue that a new phase of capitalist expansion is being prepared which, if successful, will partially change the context and dynamic for the expression of racism. In addition to (and partly instead of) people moving around the world to provide labour power in the countries where capitalism first developed, factories are now increasingly being moved to places whose populations are, so far, not drawn directly into capitalist relations of production.

The migration of New Commonwealth labour to Britain

The presence in Britain of people from the Caribbean and the Indian sub-continent is often understood as the result of their own individual decision, whether it be claimed that 'they came to find work' or 'they came to live off the Welfare State'. It is true that they did freely choose to come to Britain, but that only tells us part of the story. The migration of New Commonwealth labour to Britain in the 1950s and 1960s is one instance of a wider, historical process of migration that is the consequence of the uneven development of capitalism at a global level. Once this is understood, we can then see that New Commonwealth migrants are as much the object of the forces of capitalism as are those that they leave behind and those that they come to live amongst. Migrants, by their decision to migrate, make history. Nevertheless, their decision is determined by forces over which they have no direct control.

In a sentence, the New Commonwealth migration of the 1950s and 1960s was a consequence of 'underdevelopment' and unemployment in colonial and ex-colonial societies and a shortage of labour in certain sectors of the British economy. 'Underdevelopment' had not suddenly 'developed' in these societies in the late 1940s; it had been a long-term characteristic, not least because of British colonial exploitation. Such circumstances had led to the migration of people from these areas to find work in other parts of the world. For example, large numbers of West Indians were recruited to help build the Panama canal after 1904. Migration to the United States from the Caribbean was also high until legislation was passed in 1924. In the previous century Indians had been recruited to help build and staff the railway network in East Africa. One can multiply the examples to illustrate the point that people from these colonial societies had, for many decades, found it necessary to migrate to find work, whether as indentured or as wage labourers, in other parts of the world. So, the decision to come to Britain in the 1950s requires a more precise explanation.

In the case of the Caribbean, the McCarran-Walter Act of 1952 drastically restricted migration from the West Indies to the United States and stimulated potential migrants to look for an alternative. In the Punjab, in the 1950s, increasing economic competition associated with differences in land-holdings encouraged people to migrate to find a means of earning a cash income with which to buy land and property. The construction of a large dam in the Mirpur district of Pakistan in the early 1960s stimulated another migration to Britain. 'Behind' these particular events lay poverty and unemployment, which were partly the consequence of colonial exploitation.

Britain in the 1950s was the choice of these migrants because there were vacancies for workers in hospitals, public transport, metal manufacturing, hotels, catering and the textile industry. In only two instances did employers recruit directly in the West Indies: both London Transport and the British Hotels and Restaurants Association recruited workers for particular jobs from Barbados. The bulk of the migration was an informal process rather than a result of planning by government and by employers (as happened in much of the rest of Western Europe at this time). Information about vacancies was passed on through an informal communications network, founded on a few earlier migrants who came before the Second World War and their families and acquaintances in the Caribbean and the Indian sub-continent. This ensured a continuing flow of migrants all the while vacancies existed. In some cases, this informal channel of communication was supplemented by advertisements placed in newspapers in the New Commonwealth by employers experiencing a shortage of labour. In others, employers directly manipulated the informal and family networks to satisfy their needs for labour. The migrants of the 1950s came to Britain because there was work for them to do and because they were willing – because of economic circumstances at 'home' – to become wage labourers, at least for a few years.

Despite the informality of the process, it proved a surprisingly precise mechanism to solve a problem for British capital. If one looks at the immigration statistics for West Indians in relation to the level of unfilled vacancies for the late 1950s, one finds that a fall in the number of advertised jobs was soon followed by a fall in the numbers of people entering Britain, and vice versa. Given that the primary reason for leaving the West Indies was to find a job and a wage, there should be no surprise at this close relationship. Here was an almost perfect example of the operation of the 'free' market, with supply following demand. A similar but less precise relationship can be found for immigration from the Indian sub-continent.

This relationship between labour demand and the level of migration only breaks down in 1961 and 1962. During 1961 and up until the middle of 1962, the number of people from the New Commonwealth entering Britain continued to rise, irrespective of the demand for labour. We have seen, in chapter 2, that it was the threat of immigration control that actually increased migration into Britain, breaking the link between migration and labour demand. The legislation of 1962 and the provisions of the White Paper of 1965 effectively stopped the migration of intending wage labourers from the New Commonwealth. That these provisions did not prevent the migration of intending wage labourers from Ireland demonstrates the willingness of the British state to implement and enforce racist legislation.

That New Commonwealth migration was primarily a response to labour demand in the British economy is reflected in the characteristics of the early migrants. They were mainly young people, in their late teens and twenties. From the Caribbean came roughly equal numbers of men and women, after a short period when men outnumbered women. The women were not primarily 'dependants' (e.g. wives or children) but were coming to Britain to become wage labourers in their own right.

This was not the case for migrants from the Indian sub-continent. In the 1950s, most of them were single and married men, and only in the 1960s were they joined by wives and children.

The majority of migrants from the Caribbean and the Indian sub-continent who arrived in the 1950s came with the aim of staying only a few years in Britain. Their intention was to stay long enough to earn a sum of money sufficient to improve their material and social circumstances and/or those of their families at 'home'. Many had their travel costs paid by a pooling of family resources. These were not permanent settlers by intention but, rather, were temporary migrants by choice. However, they were unable to realise their ambition and, following the legislation of 1962 and the slackening demand for labour in the 1960s, it was their dependants who came to constitute the vast majority of migrants.

These developments are illustrated in the statistics presented in table 6.1. During the second half of the 1950s, 211,640 migrants entered Britain from the New Commonwealth, a large majority coming from the Caribbean. In the next 18 months, during the agitation for and publicity about immigration control, almost as many migrants (191,060) entered Britain as in the previous five years, a large proportion of whom were from the Indian sub-continent. Following the passage of the Commonwealth Immigrants Bill through the House of Commons and up to the end of 1968, a further 266,940 migrants entered Britain. The vast majority of these were the dependants of earlier migrants, the remainder being those who received a work voucher which entitled them to enter Britain because they had a job to come to (see table 3.1, p. 46).

Table 6.1 Net inward migration from the New Commonwealth, 1955–68

	India	Pakistan	Caribbean	Total
1955–60	33,070	17,120	161,450	211,640
1961–30 June 1962	42,800	50,170	98,090	191,060
1 July 1962–December 1968	124,260	78,670	64,010	266,940
Total	200,130	145,960	323,550	669,640

Source N. Deakin, *Colour, Citizenship and British Society*, London, Panther, 1970, p. 50.

The Conservative government claimed that the Commonwealth Immigrants Act (1962) was an attempt to rationalise immigration in order to ensure that the flow of immigration was related to the needs of the British economy (in other words, to the needs of employers). This was little more than an excuse, an attempt to justify what was a piece of racist legislation. This is shown by the fact that the migration of the 1950s had been regulated by the demand for labour. It is also shown by the fact that the government's claim was not followed by the provision of resources to assist the settlement of the migrants, not only into the jobs that they came to do, but also into wider social relations. Up until the mid-1960s, no money was planned and set aside for language teaching, for new housing, for more school places for the migrants and their families (and even after the mid-1960s, the amounts of money made available were totally inadequate to the task). If the government had been seriously concerned about rationalising the immigration process, then it would have planned and regulated all aspects of the entry of New Commonwealth migrants into Britain. It would have ensured that their labour power was available to employers *and* that the accompanying social needs of the migrants were met.

By the mid-1960s, those who had arrived from the Caribbean and the Indian sub-continent as short-term migrants, intending to return 'home' after a spell of wage labour in Britain, had become more permanent *settlers*, albeit settlers who maintained a belief in the idea of return. This was partly because the government, anxious to respond to racist agitation, had enacted legislation which embodied some of the demands of the racists. That had stimulated the panic entry of dependants. It was also partly because the migrants proved unable to save the large sums of money that they had intended. The 'Mother Country', far from being a 'land of golden opportunity', was a place of long hours of work, high rents and expensive food, at least for those joining the ranks of the semi- and unskilled working class. Racism and discrimination ensured that many of them remained in those ranks. For this reason also, it became necessary for the migrant to reconsider the original intentions. The idea of return remained, but it was postponed for some time in the future. In the meantime, a wife (or, for many of the female

Caribbean migrants, a husband) would not only allow the birth of children, but would also provide company and another income. In many cases, that meant bringing to Britain a wife and children, or a fiancé, from the Caribbean or the Indian subcontinent.

The arrival and creation of migrants' families and the birth of children led to new demands for the provision of facilities. It also created a potential future addition to the ranks of the working class. Yet as the children of West Indian, Indian and Pakistani migrants grew up and were educated in the 1960s and 1970s, the level of unemployment – gradually in the 1960s and then more quickly in the 1970s – began to increase. The capitalist economy of the 1950s that had been short of labour now found itself increasingly unable to employ its working class. As we have already seen, in the struggle over access to those fewer and fewer jobs (and other facilities and resources), racism became a measure of selection within and above the working class. By the 1970s, the cycle of capitalist production had turned full circle and prominent amongst the victims of crisis were the children of those whose labour had been so urgently required in the 1950s. The latter were also hit by unemployment.

Capitalism and labour migration in Britain

The New Commonwealth migration of labour to Britain in the 1950s represents a new phase of a process of labour migration which can be traced back into British history. The history of labour migration is an integral part of the history of the development of capitalism. That development involved the breaking up of dispersed agricultural settlements as commodity production increasingly became organised in a small number of centres, where large numbers of people became concentrated in towns. This development, already evident in the sixteenth century, was at first small-scale and local: those who migrated usually only moved small distances. This migration, from rural settlements to growing urban centres of factory production, therefore occurred within the boundary of the nation-state, although there are important exceptions. Indeed, much of the migration in the late eighteenth and early nineteenth centuries was within the confines of county boundaries. Viewed from this perspective, the New Commonwealth migration of the 1950s and 1960s indicates the growing internationalisation of the forces of capitalism: in the twentieth century, wage labour is recruited from not only within the national boundary, but also from other nation states.

Whether internal or international, these migrations were ultimately induced by the creation of a relative surplus population in one geographical location and by the demand for wage labour in expanding urban centres of capitalist production. In all cases, what the migrant was seeking by means of geographical mobility was a job and a wage. Where that search was successful, it entailed the migrant entering the ranks of the urbanised working class. In this sense, the migration of the dispossessed rural producers from Kent or from the Scottish Highlands is little different from the migration of the small-scale Sikh peasant producer or the under- or unemployed Caribbean town-dweller. All entered the urban areas of Britain, the location for the expansion of capitalism, for the sake of capital and for the sake of their own material survival. That the New Commonwealth migration has had very different political repercussions should not blind us to these underlying connections between labour migration and the development of capitalism.

Labour migration and the expansion of capitalist production

This connection can be further illustrated by the examples of migration from Ireland to Scotland, and from Europe to the United States in the nineteenth century. In the former case, the expansion occurred within Britain, from Ireland into Scotland; in the latter case, the expansion was out of Europe and into North America. Both required and induced labour migrations over greater geographical distances and across political, if not national, boundaries. Of course, the nineteenth-century migration from Ireland to Scotland was, legally, an internal migration within a single nation-state, the United Kingdom. Subsequent history has demonstrated that this could not be a permanent reality. This is not least because of the uneven expansion of capitalism which meant that capitalist development in Britain required that Ireland play a dependent economic role. The labour migration from Ireland to Scotland in the nineteenth century was expressive of that uneven development.

By the Act of Union (1707) Scotland lost its political independence and joined England and Wales to form the nation-state of Britain. The Act of Union allowed the small Scottish merchant class to engage in the spoils of colonial production and colonial trade. Hence, Glasgow developed and prospered in the eighteenth century – first, as a result of the tobacco trade with the North American colonies and, later, as a result of trade with the Caribbean colonies. The transition from trade to capitalist production within Scotland came with changing relations in textile production and in the mining and processing of coal and iron ore. But for capital to dominate production, there must be a concentration of labour power in factories, mines and urban centres. Moreover, those supplying that labour power must be able to survive only by selling it for a wage: if they had had some other means of livelihood, they would not have willingly faced the terrible urban and industrial conditions of the nineteenth century. In order to understand how labour power was concentrated in the central Lowland region of Scotland, we need to consider the circumstances of the Irish economy and its relationship with that of Britain.

By the beginning of the nineteenth century, the Irish economy was divided into three sectors. In the north-east, a linen industry around Belfast constituted a foundation for the further development of textile production and, later, industrial production. The remainder of the economy was agricultural. In the east and north, a process of land consolidation was occurring. Large farms using wage labour were being formed to supply Britain with grain and cattle. In the west and south, the economy was dominated by subsistence agriculture, the growing peasant population having to subsist on increasingly smaller plots of land. Faced with declining production and the need to obtain cash to pay rent, many peasants were forced to migrate east to work on the large farms at harvest times. Some, having reached the east coast, learnt of a similar demand in Scotland and England and they crossed the Irish Sea to work on farms for a cash wage around harvest time. Their numbers increased in the first half of the nineteenth century and, while migrating around the agricultural districts, many learnt of more permanent opportunities in the new and expanding industries. With the growth of the cotton industry in Scotland (and, slightly later, of coal and iron ore mining), there was a demand for labour. Irish peasants, faced with increased rents and even starvation, opted to become permanent wage labourers in Scotland's growing capitalist economy.

They were not alone. Handloom weavers from the Belfast region joined them as the industry declined as a result of competition with that growing in Scotland. Scottish Highlanders, who were being forced off the land as the Scottish landed aristocracy discovered what profits they could make by populating their land with sheep instead of people, were also moving into the Lowland region. They were joined by agricultural labourers from the immediate vicinity, chasing the prospect of a higher and more regular wage.

The migration of labour from Ireland to Scotland was, therefore, one element of a substantial labour migration associated with the development of capitalism. This flow of migrants was already established before the potato blight swept Ireland between 1845 and 1849, forcing hundreds of thousands of Irish peasants to choose between death or migration. Large numbers followed the well-trodden path to Scotland; others followed a new one, to the United States.

The Irish migration, in combination with that from other parts of Scotland, had real economic and political consequences for the Scottish bourgeoisie and the working class. The pool of semi- and unskilled labour increased, allowing the bourgeoisie to keep wages low – a strategy which was just one of the stimulants to working-class political action. Faced with strikes in the mining industry, the bourgeoisie occasionally replaced those outside the gates with migrants from Ireland. The large pool of labour and strike-breaking generated resentment within the working class, a resentment that was encouraged and given a precise focus by, amongst others, church ministers and newspaper editors. They drew attention to the fact that the Irish migrants adhered to the Catholic religion and were now living in a profoundly Protestant society. Attacks on Irish people and property were common throughout the middle decades of the nineteenth century, stimulated by a potent combination of material deprivation and militant anti-Catholicism. To that anti-Catholicism was wedded the idea of 'race'. The detailed history of these conflicts remains to be written, but their extent in the nineteenth century was an important factor in ensuring that the Scottish working class, particularly in the west of Scotland, developed with a clear ideological division within it.

The Irish migrants of the later nineteenth century increasingly chose the United States as their destination, in common with many hundreds of thousands of migrants from other parts of Europe. Between 1846 and 1924, some 50 million people left Europe, and about 36 million went to the United States. During the early and middle nineteenth century, industrialisation was accompanied by rapid population growth in Northern and Western Europe. In Southern and Eastern Europe, an increase in population was accompanied by increased sub-division of peasant land-holdings and the growth of a market economy, both of which decreased peasant self-sufficiency in the later nineteenth century. These combined developments were a major incentive to migration. But what was the attraction of the United States to such people?

Prior to the Civil War in the mid-nineteenth century, the United States economy was predominantly agricultural and the main motive for migration was to settle on new agricultural land. In the second half of the century, commodity production was increasingly mechanised and, by 1880, over half of the population was engaged in non-agricultural production. In this short period, handicraft production was transformed into factory production, and the demand for labour increased. There was a close correlation between the cycle of demand and the level of migration into the United States, similar to that which existed in Britain in the 1950s. The migrants, many of whom were rural peasants and lacked any industrial experience, entered the United States economy as wage labourers, doing the least-skilled manual jobs. Thus, in 1910, foreign-born workers constituted nearly half of all labourers and over one-third of machine operatives – yet they formed only a quarter of the employed population.

In the mid-nineteenth century, most of the European migrants came from Northern and Western Europe. As the century progressed, an increasing proportion came from Southern Europe. This shift in the origin of the migrants received a hostile response within the United States. It was claimed that these migrants were of a different and inferior 'race' and that their entry to the United States would lead to a 'degeneration' of the emerging American 'race'. 'Biological survival' became the theme of the agitation, and a small group of academic psychologists provided a 'respectable' leadership. Eminent academics such as Professor Robert Yerkes, Professor Carl Brigham and Professor Nathaniel Hirsch claimed that the IQ test was a suitable and accurate method of identifying 'inferior stock', arguing that 'intelligence' was biologically determined and inherited. Using data now known to be inaccurate or deliberately falsified, these psychologists used their influence to persuade both politicians and sections of the American population on the advisability of reducing immigration into the United States. Italians, Poles, Russians and Jews were among those classed as undesirable. The outcome of the agitation was the Johnson-Lodge Immigration Act (1924).

These two examples show how vast movements of people across Europe and to the United States were an integral part of the development and spread of capitalist production. They also show how the receiving countries developed a hostile political reaction, grounded on the idea of 'race'. What was common to these migrations was that predominantly rural people, subject to economic pressures, were attracted from their place of birth by the possibility of wage labour. To the migrants themselves, the migration was experienced as free. Certainly, they were not forced to migrate by political or physical pressure. Nevertheless, they made their choice only because of the impact of economic forces. They considered migration because of the difficulty of gaining a living in rural societies undergoing either development of change *and* because their labour power was in demand. The decision to migrate was made possible by the development of the forces of capitalist production, and development could continue only with an appropriate supply of labour power. We can identify a similar process at work in Western Europe after the Second World War, although the particular economic circumstances and the form of regulation of the migration were rather different.

The expansion of capitalist production in the twentieth century

Western Europe emerged from the Second World War with its economies and social organisation shattered. One of the major political concerns was that the demand for labour would not be sufficient to employ all those who survived the conflict. Throughout Europe, as a consequence, women who had been busy proving that they could do 'men's jobs' during the war were being 'persuaded' that their place was really in the home. Wage labour was again 'men's work', with certain exceptions, usually characterised by low wages.

However, as the Western European countries, generously assisted by American capital, gradually recovered and rebuilt their capitalist economies, the demand for labour increased. In the process of reconstruction, new industries and services developed, demanding new skills and offering higher wages. Electrical engineering, petro-chemicals, manufacture of new consumer goods, banking, insurance and public services all expanded dramatically during the 1950s and early 1960s. They attracted labour from other sectors of the economies, leaving the capitalists in those sectors desperately short of labour. It was not only that they could not match the higher wages. In many cases, the conditions of work were bad, the hours were long (often involving shiftwork) or unpredictable from one week to another. A shortage of labour thus appeared in certain sectors of the Western European economies.

All the major Western European economies solved the problem of selective labour shortages by encouraging labour migration, the majority of migrants being issued short-term labour contracts. They did this rather than expand the labour supply from within, by, for example, encouraging more indigenous women to enter the waged labour force. The latter solution was not preferred for the following reasons. First, it would have necessitated substantial new capital investment in child-care facilities, nursery schools and other facilities so that women – defined within dominant ideology as primarily responsible for rearing children – could make their labour power available. Second, the post-war concern about maintaining and increasing the population after the losses of the war led to a policy of encouraging the role of 'full-time' wife and mother. France even encouraged 'family' migration in line with its desire for population growth. There were other reasons, too. A major economic advantage of a migrant-labour system is that the receiving society does not have to contribute to the care or education of the migrant in his or her youth. It imports 'ready-made workers'. Finally, in those countries which operated a system of rotating migration of unaccompanied workers on fixed-term contracts, flexibility in using labour is maximised and unemployment is exported to the country of origin.

The greatest demand for labour was experienced in West Germany, France, Switzerland and Britain, although other countries have imported labour – notably, Austria, Belgium, Holland and Sweden. Italy has been both a major exporter, and more recently, an importer of labour. The shortage of labour tended to be located in the same sectors of these respective economies – notably, textiles, metal manufacture, car assembly, building, catering and hospital services. But where was the labour to come from?

There were two main sources in the 1950s. The first was the colonial and ex-colonial societies of these major European economies. The second, and the numerically predominant, was the periphery of Europe. We are here referring to a number of European societies which were both economically and geographically 'on the edge' of the Western European heartland, most of them directly fronting the Mediterranean Sea. These include Greece, Spain, Turkey, Italy, Yugoslavia, Morocco and Tunisia. Both groups of societies were characterised by their poorly-developed industrial sectors and a large population engaged in agricultural, often subsistence, production.

In some countries, such as West Germany, the recruitment and supply of workers was highly organised by the state on behalf of capital; family reunification was actively discouraged. In other cases, such as Britain and France, the greatest part of labour migration was not officially organised by the state. Nevertheless, the vast majority of migrant workers entering legally were tied to a specific job by their contract and denied political rights in the migration setting. The migrant, although a wage labourer, was therefore not a 'free' worker like those he or she might work alongside: the rights of permanent residence and political activity were denied.

Any attempt to measure the number of migrant workers in Western Europe has to face the fact that there has been a substantial clandestine migration. In the case of France, the state has half-ignored this flow for those periods when the demand for labour was high. The state, however, retains, ultimate control over the migrants because, as illegal entrants, they have no rights whatsoever. By the early 1970s, there were between 9 and 11.5 million migrant workers in Western Europe, yet, by 1974, all the labour-importing countries had virtually banned the entry of any new workers from outside the confines of the European Community. Why did this happen? Officially the ban is explained by the 'oil crisis' and the subsequent downturn in Western European economies. There are, though, at least three other reasons which demand serious consideration. First, long before the doors were slammed it was evident that, wherever possible, migrant workers were becoming settlers and beginning the process of family reunification in the migration setting – thus undermining the major economic advantages of the migrant-labour system. Second, the increasing militancy and demands for higher pay and civil and political rights by migrants must also be considered. Finally, and not unrelated to the latter point, the search for a cheap, flexible and 'docile' labour force was turning more and more to the newly industrialising nations of the Third World, a development we consider in the next section.

By 1977, a further 1 million 'temporary' workers had departed or been expelled due to the recession. However, they had been replaced in number by wives, husbands and children admitted under regulations allowing family reunification. Any new 'foreign' entrants to the labour market are now drawn from this settler population, supplemented by refugees and illegal entrants. Thus a proportion of the migrants have become relatively permanent 'residents' because they occupy positions in the labour market which, even in recession, indigenous labour is unwilling to occupy and/or which are central to the continuing operation of the capitalist economy (e.g. the transport industry). Since 1976, it has been increasingly difficult to deport migrants just because they become unemployed. Nevertheless, those who do not occupy a more central and permanent position in the capitalist economies are those who continue to pay

the price for capital's need for flexibility, evidenced by stag-
geringly high levels of unemployment amongst migrant workers
who also provide a convenient scapegoat for the problems
attendant upon recession. As some countries introduce, and
others step up, programmes of 'repatriation assistance', the
possibility of an enforced return constantly threatens these
settlers.

Why did the governments of the European periphery allow a
proportion of their population to migrate? Although these
societies have many diverse features, they also share a number
of more fundamental characteristics. They are societies in
which the development of industrial capitalism has been
delayed and/or has not kept pace with that in North-West Europe: their existence demonstrates that capitalism develops in an
uneven fashion. Hence, by all the standard economic criteria,
these countries are less 'developed'. Unemployment and underemployment are high. Productivity per person is low. A large
proportion of the population tries to gain a living from the land.
The population continues to increase in size. The 'development'
that has occurred has been limited and has often intensified
existing economic and social problems, either by stimulating a
movement of people off the land and into the towns and cities
where there are too few jobs, or by partly improving agricultural productivity, and so reducing the demand for agricultural
labour. Faced with such problems and the consequent political
agitation by the victims of 'underdevelopment', the governments of the European periphery viewed the export of people
as contract labourers as some sort of solution. They believed
that it would allow a temporary physical removal of a proportion of their populations, reducing internal political pressures
and bringing certain economic benefits. They believed labour
migration would increase foreign exchange (because the
migrants send back a proportion of their earnings) and would
introduce new skills and enterprise when the migrants returned.

It would seem that few of these 'benefits' have been realised
in practice. In the case of Turkey, it is true that the export of
labour has increased foreign exchange and has ensured that a
larger proportion of its population is employed. However, it has
also meant the migration of the skilled employed as well as the
unskilled unemployed. It is the former who tend to become

more permanent migrants, while the returned migrants bring few skills because they have been doing unskilled and semi-skilled jobs (and when they do return with sufficient money to establish a business, they normally invest in the service sector of the economy or buy land and set themselves up as small farmers).

In fact, the overall result of the migration of Turkish labour has been to increase the dependence of the Turkish economy upon the economies to which it has exported labour. Turkey has become dependent upon both foreign exchange from migration and upon the dominant economies for the employment of a significant proportion of its population. The 'prosperity' of the Turkish economy, such as it is, is dependent upon the prosperity of the labour-importing economies. When the latter go into recession, the effects echo back into the Turkish economy – leaving it with more unemployed, both in the form of prospective migrants unable to migrate and actual returned migrants. The real victims are not, however, the dependent economies of the periphery, but, rather, the migrant workers forced to return and those unable to do so: they pay the price for capitalist crisis by being confined to relative economic 'backwardness'.

We must briefly note that not all migrations are induced by primarily economic relations. Some are determined by predominantly political and ideological relations. There are a variety of economic and political circumstances which lead to the creation of political refugees and to their migration. What is relevant in this context is that changing political conditions, within national boundaries, can result in a population being defined, or defining itself, as illegitimate residents. This process can lead to their being excluded from certain rights and/or economic resources or expelled from the nation-state. Racism can play a central role in this exclusion, as was seen in the case of the Jews in Germany in the 1930s and 1940s. Not only were the Jews reduced to second-class citizens, but governments of several European countries proved themselves unwilling to admit them as refugees. In the post-1945 period, several groups of political refugees have attempted to gain entry to Britain. In the case of Kenyan Asians holding United Kingdom passports in 1968, the Labour government introduced racist legislation to prevent their entry as of right. In an amended form, this legislation later prevented Ugandan Asians gaining entry as of right when they were expelled. Provision was made for entry by a quota system, while after 1971, Australian citizens, for example, who had at least one parent or grandparent born in Britain, had the right of entry and settlement. Other political refugees allowed to enter Britain since 1945 include Hungarians, in the mid-1950s, and Chileans and Vietnamese, in the 1970s.

Towards a new international division of labour

The post-1945 expansion of capitalist production was accompanied by a further internationalisation of the labour market. Unable to supply their capitalist economies with labour power from within their national boundaries, the nation-states of the dominant economies turned to the peripheral European and ex-colonial societies for labour power to ensure the expansion of production. As far as the supply of labour was concerned, the significance of national boundaries was thereby reduced. But national distinctions increased in importance when it came to the rights and welfare of those persons supplying that labour power. The migrants *became* wage labourers but *remained* Turks, Greeks and Slavs. What capital wanted in the first instance was labour power; it did not want the people themselves – hence their secondary political and legal status. This state-defined status has proved to be a foundation for the subsequent mobilisation of opposition to the presence of migrant workers in all the dominant European societies, an opposition that is commonly expressed in terms of the idea of 'race'.

The migrant-labour solution to the post-1945 problems is, when considered in a wider context, only temporary and partial. This is so, first, because of the growing concentration of capital in the form of international companies and, second, because of capitalism's inbuilt tendency to undergo periodic crises. The post-war expansion of the Western capitalist economies has been accompanied by continuing rationalisation and take-overs, all in the pursuit of profit. The big international firms now dominate the world economy, operating in many nation-states and having a turnover which is greater than the Gross National Product of many of the smaller nation-states. The investment decisions of these massive concentrations of capital have substantial effects on national capitalist economies, not least on the employment of their populations. What we have recently witnessed is a change in the geographical location of their new investment, away from the birthland of capitalism and into the 'Third World'. This process is linked to the second factor, that of capitalist crisis. The ever-deepening crisis that began in the late 1960s has involved a combination of declining profitability and massive investment in new technology to maintain or improve international competitiveness. In order to reduce costs, the new technology partially replaces skilled labour power with machines (witness the 'revolution' in car production). Costs can be further reduced if the semi- and unskilled labour power that is combined with those new machines can be bought even more cheaply. That is possible if the capital is invested, not in North-West Europe, but in the Far East, Africa and South America. The current tendency of capitalist expansion is for capital to migrate to labour. One consequence is structural unemployment in the birthlands of capitalism.

The process can be illustrated with the example of West German companies producing textiles and clothes. A sample of 214 textile and 185 clothing companies showed that, by 1974–5, about 100 of each had subsidiary companies producing abroad. About half of these subsidiaries were to be found in the 'developing' countries and half in other 'fully' industrialised countries. These subsidiary companies more than doubled the number of workers they employed between 1966 and 1974–5. Employment in West Germany by these same companies fell about a quarter in the same period. In 1974–5, about 300,000 workers were employed in West German textile and clothing companies, producing commodities either solely or predominantly for the West German market. An analysis of the workforce of these foreign subsidiaries in the 'developing' countries showed that about 43 per cent were below the age of 20 and more than 90 per cent were female.

A new international division of labour is beginning to emerge, breaking down the division initiated in the seventeenth century between a few developed capitalist economies and those whose main role is the supply of agricultural products and raw materials. The latter are now becoming the sites of manufacturing production, linked together to produce collectively manufactured commodities for sale in the capitalist economies of the 'centre'. African and Far Eastern societies have become part of this new international division of labour because they can provide a large supply of very cheap labour, to be combined with massive capital investment. This labour can be profitably exploited as wage labour because the work process in manufacturing industries is highly fragmented and the few skills required can be taught with a minimum input of time and money. Moreover, the current technological revolution has cheapened and speeded up communication processes and transportation. In sum, increasing structural unemployment in Western Europe and North America and expanding production in Africa, the Far East, etc., are inextricably connected, integral to the continuing reproduction of capitalism. These developments have not eliminated the need for labour migration within Western Europe, but its significance for capitalism on an international scale is now much reduced.

We anticipate that these changes will be refracted in the emergence of a new form of racism. Its object will be the wage labourers recently recruited into the employ of capital in the 'Third World' economies. Again, 'they' will be accused of taking 'our' jobs, and 'they' will be described using a new version of an older imagery. In the case of the Far East, the image of the 'Oriental coolie' will take on a new significance, but one that is still linked with the idea of 'race'. Like other racisms, this one will half-grasp the changes taking place in the operation of capital but will mistakenly attribute those changes to the supposed characteristics of those newly employed as wage labour. 'Their' inferiority will be measured by an alleged willingness to sell themselves cheap and will be linked with alleged inherent characteristics of low intelligence and cunning. What the idea of 'race' obscures is the real historical development of capital, with its changing demands and strategies. Thus, while big capital extends its operations on an international scale, taking little note of national boundaries, racism becomes another link in the chain which binds the working class in Britain to its national boundaries, to its national state and ruling class and, consequently, to a reformist and, in certain circumstances, reactionary and even fascist politics. To break with racism is therefore a necessary step in the development of class consciousness and of a class struggle which adopts the same framework as capital – an international framework.

Conclusion

Labour migration must therefore be understood in relation to the expanding process of capital accumulation. Two features of the latter require particular emphasis. The first is that, over the past three centuries, the actual number of people directly involved in capitalist production has increased. Thus, the development of cotton manufacture in Lancashire in the early nineteenth century required an increase in the number of people involved in cotton production. The result was a migration of people from rural Lancashire into the growing mill-towns. In the 1950s and early 1960s, there was another expansion in capitalist production, and this opened another phase in' the history of urbanisation and proletarianisation. In this case, migrants came from the Caribbean and the Indian sub-continent to swell the working class further.

Second, the 'multiplication of the proletariat' is not a simple and even process of growth. The development of new sectors of production is accompanied by the decline of others. For example, the development and mass production of transistors meant the end of the manufacture of radio valves. Labour-intensive methods of production are constantly being replaced by more mechanised methods, a process that is also often accompanied by the reduction in the skill content of the jobs that remain. The most obvious example of this is the micro-chip revolution. These sorts of changes involve forcing people out of employment. Moreover, if new sectors of production are to develop, there must always be a potential labour force in existence. Those expelled from production and those potentially available to enter wage labour constitute the reserve army of labour. It is a necessary feature of a capitalist economy. Migration is often intimately connected with this complex of economic processes. For example, the development of new sectors of production may attract existing workers from declining sectors, leaving them with a shortage of labour which might then be filled by migrants. A good example of this is the British textile industry, which now employs large numbers of migrants from the Indian sub-continent.

These are general characteristics of a capitalist mode of production and they provide the framework which determines the process of labour migration, quite irrespective of the people who become migrants. The development of labour migration also has a number of general characteristics which require emphasis and which allow us to place labour migration in and to Britain in the wider, international context.

The first is the growing internationalisation of labour migration. The development of the world capitalist economy has as one of its features the formation of distinct nation-states. However, at the same time as national boundaries have become more fixed, movement across them has increased in response to changing labour demand consequent upon the international pattern of capital accumulation. Thus, whereas in the seventeenth and eigthteenth centuries labour immigration was a phenomenon that occurred primarily within emergent national boundaries, it is now one which is increasingly dominated by migration from one nation-state to another. In other words, the proletarianisation and urbanisation of the English rural labourer or small-holder has been replaced by the proletarianisation and urbanisation of the Pakistani rural labourer or small-holder. In the case of Germany, the equivalent is likely to happen to a Turkish rural labourer or small-holder.

Second, this internationalisation of labour migration is indicative of the uneven development of capitalism. Expressed simply, labour migration is stimulated by both the demand for labour in one geographical location and by poverty and unemployment or underemployment in others. The flow of labour therefore tends to be from undeveloped or underdeveloped regions to more developed regions – that is, areas where capitalism is most dominant and dynamic. The origin of this uneven development often lies in the very nature of capitalism, the movement and concentration of resources in particular locations by means of the market/profit mechanism. Thus, in the case of Britain (and, to a lesser extent, France and the Netherlands), labour migration since 1945 has an origin in the necessary underdevelopment of other parts of the world as a consequence of colonialism.

If these are predominantly economic processes, they cannot operate in isolation from political and ideological factors. The role of the state assumes a crucial significance when labour migration becomes internationalised. Labour-flows across national boundaries must be regulated by government policy as well as by labour demand. It is the state which sets the terms of entry, deciding which groups may enter, for how long, and under what conditions. In addition, governments, as well as other national political institutions (such as trade unions), play a major role in determining the experience and conditions of the migrants.

7. Racism and class struggle

The early chapters of this book described the nature and extent of racism within Britain; chapter 6 showed that the existence of racism as a contemporary political force can only be explained by taking note of the history of the development of capitalism and the changing international division of labour. This means, in particular, focusing upon the causes of the migration of labour and upon the causes of the political reaction to migration and to the migrants and their children by the different classes to which they come to belong. Much of the political reaction to the migrations considered in this book has been hostile, and racism has been a central component of that reaction.

We cannot assume, by definition, that such hostile political reactions are homogeneous. Rather, the opposition and hostility must, at least in part, refract the class divisions in a capitalist society. For the bourgeoisie, labour migration can be a precondition for expanded production in the context of labour shortage, or, in the context of full employment, a means of reducing wages and costs. Those sections of the bourgeoisie experiencing a labour shortage will tend to welcome migration and are unlikely to support organised opposition to it. Other sections of the bourgeoisie – those without any direct interest in labour migration – may be mobilised by such a campaign and so come to support racist demands. However, once migrants have entered the economy, a different set of forces can come into play. In some circumstances, the expression of racism within the workforce can have beneficial effects for employers insofar as it structures another division, so obstructing the development of organised working-class resistance. The expression of racism may not be at the employer's initiative, but a decision not to curb it is, in effect, an endorsement of it. There are, nevertheless, limits to the advantages of racism to employers, illustrated most clearly by instances where resistance to racism leads to industrial action on the part of those excluded. It is, therefore, because the ruling class is composed of different factions, with different interests, that we cannot assume that it will inevitably express or support racist demands.

The implications of labour migration will be quite different for the working class and its different factions. In some circumstances, labour migration can increase the total supply of labour and thus potentially lower wages and increase unemployment. In other circumstances, by relieving a labour shortage, it can assist the movement of sections of the working class into better-paid jobs. By occurring in the context of a scarcity of resources available to the working class (and capitalism has so far failed adequately to house, educate and employ the working class), labour migration can increase competition for access to those resources. Labour migration can directly affect the material circumstances of the working class in a way unique to that class.

It follows from the fact that there are different possible outcomes that racism should be viewed more as an ideology around which class struggle occurs rather than as an ideology of the ruling class. Whether or not racism is expressed by any one class, or any one faction of any one class, is a matter for historical analysis. It depends upon the historical circumstances as well as upon the particular class-nature of the society. Similarly, although migration has different implications for different classes and class-factions, it does not follow that those classes cannot constitute an alliance to oppose labour migration and the migrants that it brings. The case of Britain in the decades since the Second World War demonstrates that this is a real possibility. In this last chapter we consider the implications for class struggle of this political and ideological alliance between the state and large sections of the working class.

Racism and class formation

The vast majority of New Commonwealth migrants came to Britain to sell their labour power for a wage; the majority of these migrants and their children still do so, or, if unemployed, continue to offer their labour power for a wage. They are, therefore, part of the working class. Many of their problems and experiences are working-class problems and experiences: inflation, restrictions on trade union rights, lack of nursery facilities, poor health, systematic attempts to reduce their standard of living, and unemployment. But racism and discrimination, whether expressed and practised by the state or by sections of the working class, create additional experiences and problems. There is the problem of the disproportionate educational failure of their children in British schools, of restrictions on the entry of their wives, husbands and children into Britain, of having to produce a passport at work or on the street to prove they have the right to be in Britain, and of the risk of physical assault. So, many migrants and their children come to understand their working-class problems and experiences through their experience of racism and discrimination. A significant number are therefore taking up separate organisations and forms of struggle outside the framework of trade union organisation and electoral support for the Labour Party.

Through this complex process, a new division has been formed within the British working class, a division which, taken with all the other divisions of gender and skill, makes working-class unity both more difficult to achieve – but also even more necessary. New Commonwealth migrants and their children now tend to be viewed as a 'race' apart, rather than as an integral part of the working class. That idea (of 'race') corresponds with quite distinct material divisions within the working class. These divisions are not natural or inevitable: they are the product of human action. We now want to document some of the effects of that action.

As we have seen, New Commonwealth migrants came to Britain to fill mainly semi- and unskilled jobs that the indigenous working class had deserted in favour of others offering better pay and conditions, as well as new jobs created by the introduction of new technology and the subsequent deskilling of the workforce in certain sections of manufacturing industry. A proportion of the migrants arrived with training that suited them for skilled manual and non-manual work, but the majority of vacancies were for jobs that made little use of such abilities. Having entered the capitalist economy and the working class at this level, events conspired to keep them there.

The first was the extent of racial discrimination practised by employers, trade unions and other workers. Various studies conducted throughout the 1960s showed that discrimination in employment was widespread. It prevented these workers from moving into supervisory and administrative positions and it prevented them from moving out of semi- and unskilled manual into skilled manual labour. Migrants were therefore being restricted to the manual working class. There was, of course, some individual movement, but the vast majority stayed put. Thus confined to a specific position in the labour market, migrant labour was not directly competing with indigenous labour – at least not during the period of capitalist expansion. The second factor was the condition of British capitalism. The 1960s saw the end of the post-war boom – the very factor that had stimulated the migration. Expansion stopped and unemployment began to rise. In the absence of an expanding labour market, and in conjunction with discrimination, there was little or no room for the migrants to occupy positions further up the hierarchy of wage labour. Since the mid-1970s, when British capitalism started to restructure to increase its competitiveness in world markets, migrants have been at least equally subject to 'rationalisation' and redundancy, as the industrial and certain service sectors have had the size of their labour force reduced. A small proportion of male migrants have, however, 'escaped' from wage labour and have realised one of the traditional aspirations of certain sections of the working class: that of setting up a small business. The most well known are restaurants, newsagents, textile manufacturing and clothing. However, migrants have also set up businesses to supply goods and services specifically required by their fellow-migrants – for example, grocers, record shops, travel agents and even banking facilities. In many cases, the new class-position of these male migrants has involved the use of female migrant labour, particularly within the extended family, a precondition of which has been, and is, the ideological dependency of the latter within patriarchal relations.

A proportion of this petit-bourgeoisie has built up, over time, large sums of capital through international trading and/or multiple shop/restaurant ownership and probably now constitutes a fraction of the capitalist class proper in Britain. An article in the *Director* in June 1983 identified four Asian-owned, large-scale businesses as representative of this fraction of the bourgeoisie.

For example, the holding company, House of Sethia, is engaged in international trade, insurance and manufacturing, and has a turnover of around £100 million a year. R.K.Bagri owns a firm called Metdist which is also engaged in international trade, with a turnover of £55 million a year. Another company, the Gomba Group, is owned by Abdul Shamji and has various interests, particularly in vehicle and truck construction. This company acquired Stonefield Vehicles, Scotland, when the company was in the hands of the receivers and has recently been involved in the purchase of hotel chains. These Asian capitalists were reported as being ardent supporters of the Conservative government led by Margaret Thatcher. Having moved into such class-positions, whether petit-bourgeois or capitalist, does not by itself constitute a barrier to the experience and some of the effects of racism and discrimination. It will, however, lessen its impact, both psychologically and materially. This is not the experience and circumstances of the vast majority of New Commonwealth migrants who remain wage labourers.

The latter group was the subject of a major research project conducted in the early 1970s to assess the extent and effects of racial discrimination. Despite the fact that racial discrimination in many (but not all) areas had been made illegal, the study found that the level of discrimination was almost as high in the 1970s as it had been in the 1960s. The only major difference was that it was less overt. Moreover, the study showed that New Commonwealth migrants actually underestimate the extent of discrimination. The research also provided a great deal of evidence about the jobs and housing conditions of New Commonwealth migrants.

Male New Commonwealth migrants were overwhelmingly concentrated in manual jobs, whereas 40 per cent of the indigenous male working population were in professional management and white-collar jobs (compared with 16 per cent of New Commonwealth migrants). Although over 40 per cent of New Commonwealth male migrants were in skilled manual jobs, a further 30 per cent plus were in semi- and unskilled manual jobs. In the case of male Pakistanis and Bangladeshis, 58 per cent were in these last two categories of manual work. The same pattern applied to female migrants, although the degree of difference between them and indigenous female labour was less.

There were further, related differences in employment. For example, 31 per cent of New Commonwealth migrants were working shifts, compared with 15 per cent of indigenous workers. When earnings were compared, male New Commonwealth migrants earnt less than indigenous workers, although female wages were all equally lower than those of men. Concerning both recruitment and promotion, employers were shown to give preference to indigenous workers.

This evidence clearly shows that New Commonwealth migrants are concentrated in the manual working class and that discrimination is an important mechanism which keeps them in that position in the labour market. But they have also been over-represented in the reserve pool of labour, amongst the unemployed. Although in periods of national, full employment, levels of unemployment amongst migrant and indigenous workers are similar, in periods of capitalist crisis when the labour market is restructured, the proportion of unemployed New Commonwealth migrants increases much more rapidly than the proportion of indigenous workers. The National Dwelling and Housing Survey conducted in the autumn of 1977 showed that 9.6 per cent of New Commonwealth migrants and their children were unemployed, compared with 5.2 per cent of the general population. Moreover, analysis of changes in the registered, male unemployed amongst this group as a proportion of the total male unemployed for the late 1970s shows that, as total male unemployment rises, the rate for male New Commonwealth migrants and their children rises faster. The same evidence also shows that the level of unemployment amongst young people of West Indian origin, both male and female, and amongst women of Pakistani and Bangladeshi origin, is even higher.

A study of the unemployed conducted in spring 1979 showed that long-term unemployment tends to characterise semi- and unskilled manual work. Hence, part of the explanation for this higher rate of unemployment is that the migrants and their children are over-represented in sectors of the labour market that are prone to unemployment in periods of recession and changing patterns of capital accumulation. However, this study also showed that West Indian and Asian men have much the same risk of being unemployed regardless of their qualifications or job-level, whereas for indigenous men this is not true. Moreover, a higher proportion of Asian and West Indian men had been dismissed from their previous jobs. These findings could be explained by active discrimination by employers (the survey quoted above did, in fact, show extensive discrimination at the point of recruitment). The researchers, however, did not examine whether or not this was so. The survey's central finding – that New Commonwealth migrants and their children are over-represented among the unemployed – was reinforced by a more recent analysis of the labour-market experiences of an educationally matched sample of girls over a five-year period: West Indian girls were last in the hiring queue and first in the firing queue.

Another pattern of disadvantage is revealed when we examine housing conditions, which research has found to be uniformly worse for New Commonwealth migrants than for indigenous workers. Amongst the general population approximately 50 per cent live in owner-occupied dwellings, while the remaining 50 per cent are divided equally between council-rented and privately rented tenure. This pattern is roughly shared by West Indian migrants. Amongst Asians, 76 per cent live in owner-occupied property and a further 19 per cent in private-rented occupation: only 4 per cent live in council housing. But this high level of owner-occupation is not to be equated with good-quality accommodation. Rather, the evidence shows that the Asians have tended to buy old property in the declining central districts of major cities. When we compare the type of property occupied by New Commonwealth migrants and by the indigenous population, we find much larger proportions of the former group in terraced (rather than detached and semi-detached) property, in pre-First World War property and in property whose external condition is rated as less than good. When internal conditions and facilities are compared, there are higher levels of shared dwellings and of persons per room amongst New Commonwealth migrants and a lower level of basic amenities.

The 1960s and the 1970s have witnessed the reproduction of these same experiences amongst the migrants' children. These, however, are not migrants. A large proportion of them were born in Britain and are British citizens by birth. For them, 'home' is not Barbados or Pakistan, but Britain. They grow up in the expectation of being treated as British citizens, but have to reconcile themselves to a different reality. The evidence of educational failure, particularly amongst boys of West Indian ancestry, within the British school system has called into question the attitudes of the teachers and curriculum content. Much of the evidence points to the presence of racism. Educational failure and discrimination in the labour market, against a background of deepening economic crisis, have led to very high levels of unemployment – particularly amongst West Indian, male youth. Even the Scarman Report (1981) conceded the validity of much of this evidence.

Where excluded from wage labour, these youths constitute part of the 'wageless', or sub-proletariat – a class that has grown in size dramatically since the mid-1970s. They are forced to rely on social security and whatever other source of income they can create in order to maintain themselves. What work there is is increasingly located in the 'informal', unregistered economy. This is particularly the case for migrant women and their daughters. Indigenous and migrant entrepreneurs alike often owe their petit-bourgeois class-position to the low-paid, unprotected labour of their female, migrant employees.

Because of racism and discrimination, West Indian and Asian youth face a particular experience of wagelessness, and they are likely to be amongst the last of the reserve army of unemployed labour to be recalled when capital so requires. These youths constitute one of the weakest links in the chain of control and domination. They are beyond the 'discipline' of the workplace and of workplace political organisation. They have little or nothing to lose. Surrounded by a materialism which constantly reminds them of what they do not have, the police remain the only disciplinary force to contain the revolt that may be the course of action pursued by a proportion of the wageless.

Community resistance

The economic and political disadvantages arising from racism and discrimination tend to be experienced in the more culturally homogeneous community context than in the traditional arena of class politics, the workplace. Patterns of discrimination, when combined with the distinct historical and cultural groupings within the population of New Commonwealth migrants, have together led to self-defined communities of West Indians, Indians and Pakistanis. Such communities exist independently of simple geographical concentration: areas such as Brixton, Southall and Toxteth do not have a large, majority 'black' population. However, it is within these communities that the full brunt of racism and discrimination often falls. The fire in a house in Deptford, London, in which 13 young West Indians died in January 1981, is firmly believed by West Indians in the area to have been started by a petrol-bomb attack. The prominence given to this disputed instance (the police have refused to accept that the deaths were a result of a racist attack) has served to divert public attention from the fact that such attacks are *daily* occurrences in many areas of our major cities. These are rarely mentioned and never fully documented in the national press. In addition, we have to take account of the incidence of physical assaults on migrants and their children. These attacks have become so widespread that, as we have seen, the Home Office was finally forced to recognise that they were occurring.

Much of the resistance to racism and discrimination takes the form of self-organisation and self-defence on a community basis. Action and self-defence committees are formed and reformed in the areas of residential settlement in an attempt to draw attention to the problems and to stimulate political action. In addition, self-help organisations have been set up to teach skills and to provide additional education, as well as to ensure that religious beliefs and other cultural values are passed on to British-born children. The activities of a significant proportion of these various organisations have, in the past ten years, increasingly concentrated on developing a new and positive self-identity, one which redefines the negative associations of 'race' in the direction of a positive view of 'blackness'. The form that this cultural resistance takes varies according to the origins of the migrants and political affiliation.

The Indian and Pakistani migrants came to Britain with strong, positively viewed, historical cultures which British colonialism had never succeeded in weakening or eliminating. These were not so much national as regional, religious and linguistic cultures: Sikhs distinguish themselves from Hindus, Muslims from both; Gujaratis have different cultural characteristics from Bengalis or Punjabis, as do Mirpuris from Sylhetis. Although one should not over-emphasise the strength of this, these cultures also contain within them a tradition of revolt against colonialism. In the face of racism and discrimination, these cultures have been partially transformed and have taken on a new role insofar as they constitute the basis not only for a positive self- and community-identity, but also for political and cultural resistance. Thus, the Sikh temple becomes not simply a place of worship, but also a centre for the exchange of information and, on occasion, for political organisation. To take another example, the Indian Workers' Association, transferred from the Indian sub-continent, becomes a means of organising and defending the Indian population in a completely different context from that of India.

For the West Indian migrants, the situation was and is rather different in certain respects. The societies that developed on the various Caribbean islands were the products of colonialism and slavery and of resistance to slavery. Colonialism, in practice, meant literally wiping out the indigenous populations and, on the foundation of the exploitation of slave labour, a very particular type of society was created. It was a society in which blackness was taken as a sign of inferiority, grounded in the economic and political subordination of those enslaved, and in which all that was British and 'white' was defined as superior. Similarly, there was a tradition of revolt against slavery and colonialism, but it was always countered by a combination of complicity and pragmatic acceptance. A large proportion of the West Indian migrants arrived in Britain, half if not fully believing British colonial ideology, and expecting to be treated like all other British citizens. Their experience to the contrary has lead to an ongoing re-evaluation of the nature of British 'justice', 'democracy' and 'tolerance'.

Cultural resistance to racism and discrimination takes many forms. In a society where racism takes the form of demanding that 'they' become like 'us', the wearing of 'traditional' dress becomes laden with political significance. The case of the Sikhs is a good example. For Sikhs, the turban is one of five items of religious significance. Many Sikhs, upon arrival in Britain, chose or were forced to stop wearing turbans in order to indicate their willingness to 'integrate'. However, their compliance did nothing to prevent them from being the object of racism and discrimination. In response, they have reacted by reasserting and strengthening their commitment to Sikhism. As a result, they have insisted on their right to wear a turban at all times and have organised politically to defend that right.

The development of Rastafari amongst young West Indians in Britain is another example. Rastafari has received increasing media attention in recent years, some of it falsely suggesting a direct relationship between the movement and criminal activity. At one level, Rastafari is a religious movement which radically reinterprets the Bible: Africans are God's chosen people whom God has punished through slavery and life in Babylon. It literally creates another reality in which Rastas can live out their lives, protected both psychologically and socially from a society which rejects them and which they then reject in turn. For many young West Indians, the intense religious meaning is secondary to its secular implications of resistance and revolt – not least as expressed in the music of reggae. For all West Indians whose lives are shaped by it, Rastafari means a new and positive way of living, dressing and even walking, all of which explicitly reject the racist image of the West Indian.

A further dimension to community resistance became evident in a series of industrial disputes in the 1970s, the most notable being at Mansfield Hosiery Ltd, Imperial Typewriters, and Grunwick Film Processing. These all arose out of discrimination practised by management, coupled with trade union complicity in that discrimination or a failure to provide an organisational means of protest. Asian workers, predominantly women, were forced to take industrial action on their own initiative and without the initial support of a trade union. In the case of Mansfield Hosiery and Imperial Typewriters, Asian workers found themselves in conflict with their trade union and their fellow-workers. In all three cases, they stood firm and fell back on the financial and moral support of their local communities in order to sustain their action. Collectively, the disputes demonstrated the practical importance of community organisation and support, and that Asian women should not be stereotyped as necessarily passive and subservient.

Finally, there is resistance through riot. Riots are always the expression of deep frustration and opposition to disadvantage, and have a long tradition among the British working class. The events of the 1980s open a new chapter in a well-established story. The immediate flashpoint for the recent riots (in Bristol in 1980 and in most major English cities in 1981) has been the relationship between the wageless youth and the police, a relationship which is the product of economic deprivation and racism. Street life makes anyone the object of police attention, but racism within the state marks out the children of migrants for very special attention. A long history of police harassment brought its inevitable consequence in 1980 and 1981, though the resulting riots were fuelled by the much wider resentments and experience of repression outlined in earlier chapters .

Community organisation and cultural resistance tend to constitute the dominant forms of political response to the specific pressures and problems faced by West Indian, Indian and Pakistani workers and their children in Britain. Indeed, with unemployment amongst these workers and their children running at a much higher level then amongst the rest of the working class, such forms of organisation and resistance are often the only possible forms. They have all occurred outside the traditional framework of British working-class politics, that of political party and trade union organisation (although the strength of community is well known to certain sections of the working class). The activity of these workers is a means of both defence and attack on the ideology and practice that confines them to an inferior political and economic position, not only within British society, but also within the working class. It is, therefore, political. Moreover, it brings groups of migrants and their children into direct conflict with institutions that play a key role in maintaining hegemony and domination over the working class as a whole, not least the state.

The Labour Party and the trade union movement will, in the face of past experience, continue to be regarded with suspicion by West Indian and Asian workers and activists until their apparent mid-1970s 'change of heart' is proved in practice by a principled and concerted attack on racism and discrimination. To date, the changes, welcome though they are, have occurred as the result of fears about the electoral success of the National

Front and the declining electoral fortunes of the Labour Party.

The significance of community struggles should not completely divert attention from involvement in other forms of struggle and from the class divisions that are clearly emerging amongst these populations of migrant origin. New Commonwealth migrants have played an active role in various traditional working-class organisations and forms of struggle, a role which reflects important parallels in political consciousness with 'indigenous' workers – parallels which originate in the common position and experience of wage labour. The most recent evidence of this is found in the industrial disputes which have occurred in the public sector since the 1970s, especially in the National Health Service. Widespread trade union organisation of migrants and their active participation in trade union struggles can be contrasted with the growth of not only a petit-bourgeoisie but also a bourgeoisie amongst these populations of migrant origin. The latter entails the creation of quite distinct economic and political interests, not least an interest in the maintenance of capitalist relations of production.

Racism and class struggle

Whatever criticisms may be made about the way in which these community struggles are interpreted, one cannot deny their reality, nor their origins in racism and discrimination. The continuing expression of racism, the growing strength and influence of those actively seeking the implementation of a policy of 'repatriation', the intensification of material inequalities and the continuing economic crisis, all suggest that these forms of struggle will continue. As struggles of either a fraction of the working class or of the sub-proletariat, they are necessarily a dimension of the class struggle.

But the experience and effects of racism do not alter the general class-position of those who are its object. Racism may be one of the means through which class-exploitation is experienced and the struggle against racism may be one form of struggle against capitalist domination – but these can never be autonomous or isolated from other means of exploitation and struggles against capitalism. For instance, migrant women experience racism on the same daily basis as migrant men.

However, racist oppression is shaped and experienced for them in a particular way because they share with all women subordination as a gender. This dual oppression further confines migrant women and their daughters to certain types of work and reinforces their exploitation as waged workers. But by virtue of being a wage labourer, the West Indian or Asian migrant, or a descendant of such a migrant, whether male or female, also shares with other fractions of the working class a range of economic, political and ideological pressures. For example, both the migrant and the indigenous worker have had to cope with the rationalisation of production and attempts to weaken the trade union movement, both have had to respond to divisions within the Labour Party and the electoral success of a right-wing Conservative Party, and both have had to react to the messages contained in the press and other forms of mass media. The realities of unemployment, declining wages, reduced social service and National Health provision and an elitist education system are to some degree experienced by all fractions of the working class.

Those who sell their labour power for a wage are required to deal with these problems in the present period because it is this class which bears the brunt of the current efforts to make capitalism in Britain more internationally competitive. Hence, a common class-position means that the political consciousness and action of all those who occupy those positions are open to similar influences. Thus, a study which we conducted in the mid-1970s showed that the political consciousness of a group of semi-skilled manual, indigenous and West Indian workers, both male and female, contained many common elements. The workers we interviewed shared certain beliefs about the nature of class structure and the exercise of power in Britain, about political parties and about the nature and role of trade unions. These shared elements of political consciousness reflected a shared experience of being a wage labourer.

Such continuities in political consciousness have been reproduced in trade union struggles, notably in various sectors of state employment, particularly the National Health Service, where migrant and indigenous workers can be found. These struggles show that racism does not structure all situations on all occasions. Although it is an ever-present possibility, West Indian, Asian and indigenous workers do work and live side by side without their personal relations being continually disrupted by racism, and it is out of such circumstances that united struggles at grassroots level can and do develop. At the very local level, both in the workplace and residentially, the shared experience of, for example, intransigence by managers or council officials leads to collective action by indigenous and West Indian and Asian workers. Amongst the sub-proletariat, the same applies. What was significant about the riots in Toxteth, Liverpool, in 1981, was that they were a conflict between the police and a cross-section of the population of an area facing massive unemployment and material decline. That population included both indigenous people and the descendants of earlier Caribbean migrants.

Although racism does have the effect of fragmenting and disorganising the working class, this is neither complete nor permanent. The very nature of capitalism ensures that the working class, including all its fractions, is subject to a common process of exploitation. This common class-position constitutes the foundation for the development of general class struggles, involving several class factions. However, the specific conditions for the widespread emergence of such a struggle against racism do not currently exist. Racism remains a not insignificant dimension of state practice and Conservative government strategy, while the explicit right-wing nationalism, which has proved electorally so effective, openly excludes 'alien cultures' from its view of British national identity. For both the state, and sections of the working class, racism can be used to help both understand and define a strategy to find a solution to the current crisis. Certainly, the forces of the far right have never been as strong as they are now since the 1930s. And, equally significant, the record of the trade union and labour movement regarding racism over the previous quarter of a century means that it faces major difficulties in presenting itself as an effective, anti-racist force. How can we link anti-racist struggles with more general ones?

The Labour Party and the trade unions must mobilise their rank and file against racist practices at all levels; they must also reverse all those policies which have led to and have endorsed state racism. It is because, as we have shown, the Labour Party was one of the main architects of the institutionalisation of racism by the state that this reversal of policy must be principled and thorough. The Labour Party's ability to carry through such a mobilisation and reversal of policy is a matter of debate.

The other potential vehicle for the required initiatives are the various revolutionary socialist organisations. While these organisations have a more consistent record of anti-racist activity and support for struggles of the racialised factions of the working class, their influence is very limited and has shown few signs of growing dramatically in the course of the deepening crisis.

There is a further factor to be considered when discussing the possibility of the development of more unified class struggles out of fragmentation and disorganisation. We have consistently stressed the importance of migration to the formation and reproduction of the working class, but migration is not always one-way. The migration process, viewed from the perspective of the migrant rather than from the workings of capitalism, is one which does not necessarily involve the breaking of all links with the place and country of origin. These continuing links can be both social and economic. Thus, the migrant may have relatives in the place of origin; he or she may also continue to own land or some form of small-scale capital and, indeed, the migration may be induced by a desire to expand and enlarge that land or capital ownership. In such circumstances, migration and proletarianisation are, from the perspective of the migrant, no more than a means to improve a petit-bourgeois class-position in the place of origin. Here we have an example of migration placing people in two different class-locations simultaneously. Thus, the labourer in a Midlands iron foundry may also be a small landowner in Pakistan. This dual class-position may mean that commitment to working-class organisation and struggle is highly instrumental and dictated by conservative inclinations. Even where there are no continuing economic interests in the place of origin, family ties will constitute a source of an alternative cultural identity. In these various circumstances, the country of origin can be a place to which the migrant can return if the economic and/or political situation in Britain deteriorated to the point where economic aims could not be realised, or racist hostility made life very difficult. In such circumstances, a reverse migration might appear more beneficial than involvement in political struggle in Britain.

However, this is not an option open to a majority of New Commonwealth migrants and their children in Britain. First, only a minority of migrants from the Caribbean and the Indian sub-continent own land or capital in their place of origin. In the absence of such ownership, the reality of their lives as workers in Britain could only be replaced by a life as a wage labourer in the Caribbean or Indian sub-continent, and economic circumstances there are often even less certain than in Britain. Second, after some 20 years or more in Britain, the migrants have made a wide range of material and emotional investments in Britain: they have become, in effect, settlers. Third, and most significant, their children are not migrants. Most of them have been born in Britain and it is to a position within the British class structure that they will be allocated in the first instant, whether it be the working class or the sub-proletariat. Indeed, it is because New Commonwealth migrants and their children have become effectively a permanent addition to various positions in the British class structure that the racist right wishes to implement a policy of 'repatriation'.

A further source of fragmentation which raises even more complex issues is the development of a migrant petit-bourgeoisie whose conditions of existence include the employment of fellow-migrants as wage labourers. This is particularly common in the clothing industry. Moreover, the petit-bourgeoisie is predominantly male, while those selling their labour power are mainly women, often receiving very low wages for long hours of work in very inferior working conditions. Finally, patriarchal elements in the particular migrant cultures are used to discipline and control these mainly female workforces. Yet this complex of class and sexist exploitation occurs in a context where at least a proportion of the petit-bourgeois entrepreneurs have chosen this form of economic activity as a consequence of the effects of racism and discrimination. The 'small business' is a way of avoiding at least some of the racist pressures and can be initiated with redundancy money or accumulated family savings from wage labour. This strategy is also encouraged by the current Conservative government as part of its 'free enterprise' ideology to solve the problem of 'inner-city' decline.

Nevertheless, it is around the 'repatriation' initiative and the ongoing experience of racism and discrimination that political struggle will continue in the immediate future. These are important dimensions of the class struggle. The activities of the racist right are encouraged by the existence of a right-wing Conservative govenment attempting to solve an economic crisis of capitalism by means of an ideological offensive based around a notion of British nationhood anchored in the colonial past. The ideas of 'race' and 'law and order' now play a central ideological role in the struggle to restore capitalist profitability. On the other hand, the continuing expression of racism and practice of discrimination will necessitate the continuation of the various struggles of the migrants and their children. In the longer term, there is the possibility that the changing international division of labour, a consequence of the large-scale export of capital to establish sites of capitalist production in parts of the 'Third World', will mean that large-scale unemployment in Western Europe will become permanent. This would mean not only an end to labour migration within Europe – it would also almost certainly provide the foundation for a renewed racist initiative, against both 'Third World' workers abroad and in European cities. In such circumstances, the final racist demand for a 'white man's Britain' would make an even greater appeal to a common sense grounded in the belief in the reality of 'race'.

One of our major objectives in this book has been to show that this common sense is fundamentally mistaken. In order to contest it, it is necessary to remember that New Commonwealth migrants have been men and women responding to the demand for labour by British capitalists. They have had to migrate in order to become wage labourers in Britain. Neither their presence, nor their physical or cultural characteristics, induces any new division within British society. What has led to a division, particularly within the working class, is the political reaction to their migration, and to their physical and cultural characteristics. The further fragmentation of the working class is the combined result of various activities of the state, employers, trade unions and workers who have expressed racist ideas and practised discrimination. Hence, the political problem is neither 'race relations' nor immigration. It is not a problem of 'colour'. The problem is the racism that is generated in a capitalist society in which both people and wealth are forced to migrate for the sake of profit alone.

Postscript

Soon after this book was finished, the campaign by the far right of the Conservative Party to persuade the Conservative government to implement a policy of 'voluntary repatriation' achieved further success. In reply to a parliamentary question on 19 January 1984, by Harvey Proctor MP, David Waddington, Minister of State, revealed that the government's review of the 'repatriation scheme under Section 29 of the Immigration Act (1971), was complete and had resulted in a number of changes. These changes ease considerably the conditions under which the state can give financial assistance to individuals who wish to be 'repatriated'.

Up until now, there have been two means of providing such financial assistance. Under Section 7 of the Social Security Act (1966), the Supplementary Benefits Commission has had the power to make a single payment to assist 'immigrants' to return 'home' where there was no prospect of self-support, either because the individual was permanently ill or permanently unemployable and, in both cases, unable to pay for the journey. Under Section 29 of the Immigration Act (1971), the Home Secretary has had the power to make payments to individuals and members of their family or household who wish to live permanently elsewhere. This scheme has been administered by the International Social Service organisation.

On 19 January, David Waddington informed Harvey Proctor that the former scheme will be absorbed into the latter, that the requirement that the applicant must have a poor record of employment will be abolished, and that the qualification that the applicant must have 'failed to settle' in Britain will no longer apply. In addition, the earnings limit for those in work will be raised from £5 to £20 above supplementary benefit level (*Times*, 20 January 1984). In the context of Margaret Thatcher's claims about 'swamping', the intensified campaign by the far right of the Conservative Party for an active policy of 'repatriation' (which was unsuccessfully debated at the 1983 annual conference of the Conservative Party), and the increasing level of violence against migrants and their children, this is a significant concession to the racist lobby. As Fiona Mactaggart, general secretary to the Joint Council for the Welfare of Immigrants, put it (*Times*, 20 January 1984):

> It seems to reflect a general attitude of this Government that the presence of the immigrant community is not particularly welcome here and that it will take steps, which can be seen as respectable, to remove them from here if that is possible. This is one of those steps.

Guide to reading

For each chapter of the book, we list below a number of accessible books which deal in greater detail with the major themes. We also list the most important specific references to empirical evidence.

Preface

A series of articles on the Conservative government and its policy since 1979 can be found in S.Hall and M.Jacques (eds), *The Politics of Thatcherism*, London, Lawrence & Wishart, 1983. The British political reaction to the Falklands crisis in 1982 is discussed in A.Barnett, *Iron Britannia*, London, Allison & Busby, 1982.

Chapter 1

The argument of this chapter is more fully developed in R.Miles, *Racism and Migrant Labour*, London, Routledge & Kegan Paul, 1982. The first half of M.Barker, *The New Racism*, London, Junction Books, 1981, develops the argument about the changing content of racism. That the idea of 'race' has a particular historical origin is explained in M.Banton, *The Idea of Race*, London, Tavistock, 1977. The UNESCO statements on the status of the 'race' idea can be found in A.Montagu, *Statement on Race*, London, Oxford University Press, 1972. A powerful description of racism in England is offered by A.Dummett, *A Portrait of English Racism*, Harmondsworth, Penguin, 1973.

Pages 2–3 Powell's infamous speeches of 1967–8 are collected, with a commentary, in B.Smithies and P.Fiddick, *Enoch Powell on Immigration*, London, Sphere, 1969.

Page 3 The quote from T.Nairn is from his *The Break-up of Britain*, London, Verso, 1981, p.274.

Page 8 The mass media study is P.Hartmann and C.Husband, *Racism and the Mass Media*, London, Davis-Poynter, 1974.

Page 11 The interview quotation is from A.Phizacklea and R.Miles, *Labour and Racism*, London, Routledge & Kegan Paul, 1980.

Chapter 2

A useful factual account of post-war labour migration to Britain can be found in the appendices to Unit of Manpower Studies, *The Role of Immigrants in the Labour Market*, London, Department of Employment, 1977. Another account, dealing with Western Europe as a whole, is S.Castles and G.Kosack, *Immigrant Workers and Class Structure in Western Europe*, London, Oxford University Press, 1973.

The development of the 'race/immigration' theme in British politics can be traced in the columns of *Hansard* which records debates and questions in the House of Commons. We make extensive use of this source in this and the following two chapters. For other accounts, see E.J.B.Rose and others, *Colour and Citizenship*, London, Oxford University Press, 1969; P.Foot, *Immigration and Race in British Politics*, Harmondsworth, Penguin, 1965; and I.Katznelson, *Black Men, White Cities*, London, Oxford University Press, 1973; S.Josh; and B.Carter, 'The Role of Labour in the Creation of a Racist Britain', *Race and Class*, 1984, xxv(3), pp 53–70. For trade union attitudes and practices, see R.Miles and A.Phizacklea, *The TUC, Black Workers and New Commonwealth Immigration, 1954–1973*, Research Unit on Ethnic Relations Working Paper no. 6, Birmingham, University of Aston, 1977. An assessment of the social capital requirement of migrant labour since 1945 can be found in K.Jones and A.D.Smith, *The Economic Impact of Commonwealth Immigration*, Cambridge, Cambridge University Press, 1970.

Page 20 Details of the number of working days lost through strikes and industrial accidents are in R.Hyman, *Strikes*, London, Fontana, 1972, p. 34.

Page 24 Royal Commission on Population, Cmnd. 7695, HMSO, 1949.

Page 40 The relationship between labour demand and West

Indian migration is documented in C.Peach, *West Indian Migration to Britain*, London, Oxford University Press, 1968. Details of the Gallup Poll results for this period can be found in D.T.Studler, 'British Public Opinion, Colour Issues and Enoch Powell: A Longitudinal Analysis', *British Journal of Political Science*, 1974, 4, pp. 371–81; and D.T.Studlar, 'Policy Voting in Britain: The Coloured Immigration Issue in the 1964, 1966 and 1970 General Elections', *American Political Science Review*, 1979, 72, pp. 46–64.

Page 44 The quotation of W.Deedes is from his *Race Without Rancour*, London, Conservative Political Centre, 1968.

Chapter 3

The additional reading suggested for Chapter 2 is relevant to this chapter. In addition, R.Moore and T.Wallace, *Slamming the Door: The Administration of Immigration Control*, London, Martin Robertson, 1974, exposes the racist nature of the law and practice of immigration control. A.Sivanandan, *A Different Hunger*, London, Pluto Press, 1982, pp. 101–40, documents the pressures leading to the institutionalisation of racism in Britain. For further material on Enoch Powell, see P.Foot, *The Rise of Enoch Powell*, Harmondsworth, Penguin, 1969.

Page 66 Political and Economic Planning (PEP) carried out research which demonstrated that discrimination was widespread in access to employment and housing. See W.W.Daniel, *Racial Discrimination in England*, Harmondsworth, Penguin, 1968.

Chapter 4

The history of the development of resistance to racism is documented in A.Sivanandan, *A Different Hunger*, London, Pluto Press, 1982, and R.Moore, *Racism and Resistance*, London, Pluto Press, 1975. More detailed information on the widening institutionalisation of racism can be found in Institute of Race Relations, *Police Against Black People*, Longon, IRR, 1978, and P.Gordon, *White Law*, London, Pluto Press, 1983. Another view of the changing expression of racism within the ruling class and the state is argued by E.Lawrence, 'Just Plain Common

Sense: The "Roots" of Racism', in Centre for Contemporary Cultural Studies, *The Empire Strikes Back*, London, Hutchinson, 1982. For an account of the state reaction to the disturbances in Bristol in 1980, see H.Joshua, T.Wallace and H.Booth, *To Ride the Storm*, London, Heinemann, 1983.

Page 80 The article by S.Hall is reprinted in S.Hall and M.Jacques (eds), *The Politics of Thatcherism*, London, Lawrence & Wishart, 1983.

Page 82 Part of the text of the NF leaflet is reproduced in D.Humphry and M.Ward, *Passports and Politics*, Harmondsworth, Penguin, 1974, p. 128.

Page 85 The details of the creation of the moral panic over 'mugging' are from S.Hall and others, *Policing the Crisis: Mugging, the State and Law and Order*, London, Macmillan, 1978.

Page 88 Lord Scarman, *The Brixton Disorders, 10–12 April, 1981*, London, HMSO, 1981 (and subsequently published by Penguin, 1982). For other reactions to the 1981 riots, see D.Cowell and others (eds), *Policing the Riots*, London, Junction Books, 1982. Police manipulation of crime statistics is discussed in M.Ramsay, 'Mugging: Fears and Facts', *New Society*, 25 March 1982, and in S.Benton, 'Mugging up the Figures', *New Statesman*, 19 March 1982.

Page 90 The Runnymede Trust report is C.Demuth, *'Sus': a Report on Section 4 of the Vagrancy Act, 1824*, London, Runnymede Trust, 1978.

Page 93 The study of racist violence is Home Office, *Racial Attacks*, London, Home Office, 1981.

Page 94 The study of the operation of the entry certificate scheme is M.Akram and J.Elliot, *Appeal Dismissed*, London, Runnymede Trust, 1977.

Page 103 Changes in the attitude and practice of the TUC are detailed in R.Miles and A.Phizacklea, 'The TUC and Black Workers, 1974–76', *British Journal of Industrial Relations*, 1978, XVI, pp. 195–207.

Page 104 Bethnal Green and Stepney Trades Council, *Blood on the Streets: A Report on Racial Attacks in East London, 1978*.

Page 107 On raids see Paul Gordon, *White Law*, London, Pluto Press, 1983, pp. 35–8 and his *Passport Raids and Checks: Britain's Internal Immigration Controls*, Runnymede Trust, 1981.

Page 112 A useful account and analysis of the riots of 1981 is in M.Kettle and L.Hodges, *Uprising!*, London, Pan Books, 1982.

Chapter 5

A readable history of the growth of the National Front is M.Walker, *The National Front*, London, Fontana, 1977. For a more recent account, see C.T.Husbands, *Racial Exclusionism and the City: the Urban Support for the National Front*, London, Allen & Unwin, 1983; also C.T.Husbands, 'The National Front: What Happens to it Now?', *Marxism Today*, 1979, September, pp. 268–75. The best analysis of the fascist nature of NF politics is found in M.Billig, *Fascists*, Harcourt, Brace, Jovanovich, 1979; see also D.Edgar, 'Racism, Fascism and the Politics of the National Front', *Race and Class*, 1977, XIX(2), pp. 111–31. The periodical *Searchlight* always contains important contemporary material on fascism and racism in Britain.

Page 124 The writer who investigated the NF is N.Fielding whose evidence can be found in *The National Front*, London, Routledge & Kegan Paul, 1981.

Page 125 Details of prosecutions of NF members and sympathisers is derived from *Searchlight*, 1982, 79, p. 4.

Page 132 For an important account of the origin and development of nationalism, see B.Anderson, *Imagined Communities*, London, Verso, 1983. See also T.Nairn, *The Break-up of Britain*, London, Verso, 1981.

Chapter 6

There is an extensive literature on the topic of this chapter: S.Castles and G.Kosack, *Immigrant Workers and Class Structure*, London, Oxford University Press, 1973; R.Miles, *Racism and Migrant Labour*, London, Routledge & Kegan Paul, 1982; C.Meillassoux, *Maidens, Meal and Money*, Cambridge, Cambridge University Press, 1981; A.Phizacklea (ed.), *One-Way Ticket*, London, Routledge & Kegan Paul, 1983; S.Castles H.Booth, and T.Wallace, *Here for Good*, London, Pluto Press, 1984. For the new international division of labour, see F.Fröbel and others, *The New International Division of Labour*, Cambridge, Cambridge University Press, 1981. An important study of the effects of the contract migrant labour scheme is S.Paine, *Exporting Workers: The Turkish Case*, Cambridge, Cambridge University Press, 1974. On labour migration in and to Britain in the nineteenth century, see A.Redford, *Labour Migration in England, 1800–1850*, Manchester, Manchester University Press, 1976; D.F.McDonald, *Scotland's Shifting Population*, Glasgow, Jackson, Son & Co., 1937.

Page 147 The history of academic involvement in racist agitation in the United States is outlined in L.Kamin, *The Science and Politics of IQ*, Harmondsworth, Penguin, 1977.

Chapter 7

In addition to the references cited for chapter 4, see also the special issue of *Race and Class*, 1981/82, XXIII (2/3).

Page 163 The large-scale study of disadvantage was conducted by PEP and later published in paperback as D.J.Smith, *Racial Disadvantage in Britain*, Harmondsworth, Penguin, 1977.

Page 164 The study of unemployment conducted in spring 1979 is published as D.J.Smith, *Unemployment and Racial Minorities*, London, Policy Studies Institute, 1981.

Page 165 The study of educationally matched school-leavers is S.Dex, 'The Second Generation: West Indian Female School-leavers', in A.Phizacklea (ed.), *One-Way Ticket*, London, Routledge & Kegan Paul, 1983.

Page 166 Since the late 1960s, there have been numerous reports and studies indicating the extent of educational failure, particularly amongst West Indian boys in the British school system. The most recent report by Rampton was *West Indian Children in Our Schools*, Cmnd 8273, London, HMSO, 1981.

Page 172 The argument about the significance of wage labour to the political consciousness of migrant workers in Britain is developed in A.Phizacklea and R.Miles, *Labour and Racism*, London, Routlege & Kegan Paul, 1980.